TANK TWINS

TWINS IN TANKS

East End Brothers-in-Arms: 1943 - 1945

by
Stephen W Dyson

LEO COOPER
LONDON

IMPERIAL WAR MUSEUM

First published in Great Britain in 1994 by
Leo Cooper
in association with the Imperial War Museum
Leo Cooper is an imprint of Pen & Sword Books Ltd,
47 Church Street, Barnsley, S. Yorkshire S70 2AS
Copyright © Stephen W. Dyson 1994

A CIP catalogue of this book is available from the British Library

ISBN 0 85052 274 9

Typeset by Yorkshire Web

Printed & Bound by
Redwood Books
Trowbridge, Wiltshire.

Dedicated to my twin brother, Thomas,
and to all those who fought with us in the battles
from the Normandy beachhead to Germany with
107 Regiment (The King's Own),
Royal Armoured Corps, 34 Tank Brigade.

Contents

Author's Note

This is a true story of the experiences and adventures of a conscript in the British Army during the Second World War.

All the named characters are real people. In other instances, individual names have not been divulged where it would be unfair to do so.

A copy of the original manuscript has been presented to the Imperial War Museum, London.

Stephen Dyson
Caterham, 1993

The Dyson family at the outbreak of war, 3 September 1939

376 Bethnal Green Road, London

Robert Dyson, age 55. My father was a man of medium height, with dark hair and a moustache. He had been a soldier in World War I, and was captured during the Battle of the Somme in 1916 and held as a POW for three years. During the Second World War he worked as a clerk in the Borough Treasurer's department of Bethnal Green Borough Council, a post which made full use of his neat handwriting and good grammar. He had a charming personality, with an even-tempered and passive nature, which meant he was sometimes a little dominated by my mother. Nevertheless he was a happy man who enjoyed his beer and cigarettes, and loved reading books.

Margaret Dyson, age 54. My mother was a full-figured woman of medium height, with shoulder-length auburn hair. She was quite a character - during the First World War she worked at Woolwich Arsenal and was a leader of demonstrations demanding better pay and conditions for women, which led to her arrest on at least one occasion. Between the two wars she worked as a bookbinder's folder, and scrimped and scraped on limited money to bring up a large family and pay for our music lessons. She was a wonderful mother, always welcoming our friends and enjoying our singalong parties.

Steve Dyson, age 23. At the outbreak of war I was a bit of a dandy, a few weeks short of my 24th birthday, and working as a buyer for a shopfitting, building and engineering group. I was of medium height, with dark hair and a pencil moustache, and weighed about 8 stone 6 pounds - I boxed as a bantamweight. My other favourite sports were football, cricket and swimming, and I also played semi-professionally in a dance band and was a good ballroom dancer. I enjoyed reading and writing, and was fond of a drink and a cigarette. I had a passive temperament, but could explode dramatically if provoked.

Tom Dyson, age 23. Tom was my twin brother, although fraternal rather than identical. He had dark hair, centre-parted like mine, but was clean-shaven. Of medium height, he weighed around 9 stone and had been a professional featherweight boxer before joining Bethnal Green Borough Council's refuse collection department. He was also a good ballroom dancer, and a talented 'by ear' pianist who entertained in pubs and clubs. He was a good leader and organiser, spontaneously witty and always the centre of attraction, but could be aggressive at times. Like me, he enjoyed football, cricket, swimming, drinking and smoking.

Eileen Dyson, age 19. My sister was a pretty girl with dark, shoulder-length hair, a slim figure, and a charming personality. She worked as a telephonist at Bethnal Green Town Hall, and enjoyed ballroom dancing in her spare time. She was also an excellent ballad singer, and led many of our singalongs.

Phyllis Dyson, age 13. My youngest sister was a slightly plump, pretty girl, with dark, shoulder-length hair and a lively, witty personality. She clowned around a lot, enjoyed ballroom dancing, and joined in our musical and theatrical activities.

Chingford, Essex

Maggie Craske (née Dyson), age 32. My eldest sister was a pretty, dark-haired woman of medium height and build, with a warm and generous personality. She worked as a seamstress in the Jewish rag trade in Bethnal Green, but lived in Essex with her husband - she was the only one of us who was married at the start of the war. She was a brilliant pianist, and had played semi-professionally with me in a dance band before the war.

Albert Craske, age 34. Maggie's husband.

Albie Craske, age 6. Albert and Maggie's son.

Hong Kong

Bob Dyson, age 30. My elder brother was a colour sergeant in the regular army, serving with the Middlesex Regiment in the Hong Kong garrison at the outbreak of war following a lengthy spell of service in the Middle East. He was still single, a dark-haired and clean-shaven man of medium height and stocky build, and a good all-round sportsman. Bob was the only one of our family who was completely uninterested in music.

Preface

During the Second World War, the whole Dyson family contributed to the war effort in their different ways.

My parents became joint honorary secretaries of the Bethnal Green Red Cross Penny-a-Week Fund, and my father shared in the fire watch rota at Bethnal Green Town Hall.

My mother joined the WVS, and participated in all the good works undertaken by that voluntary body to help victims of the blitz. In 1944 she was elected to the Borough Council. She also made several broadcasts on the BBC, having been chosen by them to represent a 'typical Londoner' in topical programmes.

Bob served in the Hong Kong garrison until he was captured by the Japanese in December 1941. He spent nearly four years in a Japanese POW camp, and was released in 1945.

In August 1941 Eileen married Dick Bridger (the son of the mayor of Bethnal Green at the outbreak of war), by special licence. Dick was posted within a few weeks, and served with the army in the Middle East and Italy until the end of the war.

Eileen carried on working at the Town Hall, and was a rota emergency air raid telephonist throughout the war, for which she was presented with a commendation certificate by the mayor.

Eileen and Phyllis became performing members of the BeeGees Concert Party, formed by staff at Bethnal Green Town Hall to raise funds for war charities.

Maggie was the stand-in pianist for the BeeGees Concert Party, and was often called upon to perform with them at short notice. She also worked for the ARP and AFS in Chingford.

This book mainly concerns the war exploits of my twin brother, Tom, and myself. We were conscripted into the army on 3 May 1940, and drafted to different regiments despite our expressed wishes to serve together. I was enlisted into the Middlesex Regiment in London's Mill Hill; Tom went to the East Surrey Regiment at Kingston in Surrey.

Fortunately for us our MP, Sir Percy Harris, intervened with the Minister for War on our behalf, and our wish to serve together was granted. We were reunited on 3 August 1940, when I was transferred to Tom's regiment, and we both became part of the 8th Home Defence Battalion East Surrey Regiment at Gravesend in Kent. Over the next two years we undertook various defence duties in the south-east corner of Kent, first with the East Surreys, and later with the Royal West Kent Regiment. In January 1942 Tom also got married, to a girl named Rose Lewis.

Despite experiencing some heavy bombing raids against vital targets we were guarding, plus blitz raids on London during official leave passes (and innumerable AWOL outings), we became bored stiff with soldiering in England. Our only personal contact with the enemy was hunting for German airmen who had baled out and parachuted down in the Kent countryside. We were thus overjoyed when, in December 1942, our battalion was put through personnel aptitude tests for dispersal to specialist units in preparation for the impending cross-Channel invasion. Tom and I were selected for tank training.

Hamburg

Bremen
Soltau
Fallingbostel
Meinersen
Gifhorn
Osnabrück   Hanover   Fallersleben
Burgsteinfurt   Minden   Lehre
Norwalde
Munster

BERLIN

GERMANY

Bocholt
Dingden
Wesel   Bochum

Rhine   Cologne

Remagen

Dresden

Nuremberg

Tongres

Liège

R. Meuse

Namur

Jeneffe   Maffe   Barvaux
Porcheresse

Dinant

Celles

Ciergnon

Ardennes

Miles
0 10 20 30

Bastogne

AUSTRIA

SWITZERLAND

ITALY

Chapter 1

The Channel Crossing

Our tanks rumbled into Fareham dockyard and halted at the top of the hards, a cobbled slope leading down to the water. There were quite a lot of ships in harbour, but we knew immediately which one we would be sailing in: it was waiting there, at the bottom of the slope, with the bow door down and the water lapping around it. It had the letters LCT (Landing Craft Tank) on its side, followed by numbers.

As my tank went up the ramp door and into the ship I could see the first three tanks secured with iron chains on the left of the craft, so our troop did likewise on the opposite side under the supervision of one of the ship's crew. I didn't know port from starboard at the time: it was left or right of the ship for me, and I bet for the majority of the tank crews. The bow door was raised back into position, and we all clambered up the iron staircase leading to the deck and leaned over the ship's rail to watch the enthralling activity going on around us.

I'd never been to sea before; in fact, the only times I'd been on water were at the oars of a rowing boat, penny rides on a motor boat around the Victoria Park lake in Bethnal Green in my childhood, and the Gravesend - Tilbury ferry. I wasn't alone, though, in wondering how the sea journey to Normandy through the choppy waters of the English Channel would affect us, and whether the pills we had been given to curb the effects of sea-sickness would prove efficacious.

Joe Whelan, at my side, drank the remains of his bottle of beer and threw the empty bottle into the water. 'This is going to be a bloody big difference to just crossing the Mersey on the ferry.' Taffy, looking a little disconsolate, said, 'I've never even been on one of them, boyo. Even the swings used to make me sick when I was a kid. Still, I've got plenty of sick bags to fill up if it comes to it.'

'Never mind, Taffy,' I said, putting my arm round him. 'There's worse things at sea than being sick: the odd floating mine, lurking U-boat, dive bomber...'

'Is that all?' said Taffy with a wry grin. 'I think I'd rather be seasick!'

'Well, you'll soon find out,' said Joe. 'We're moving.'

Sure enough, the ship began to back away slowly from the hards, swung round, and we were on our way to Normandy. We picked up speed as we steamed along, passing other ships of all shapes and sizes in the harbour, and endless lines of cranes on the docksides as we headed for the Solent. Before long we were out into open sea in the Channel, and the flat-bottomed craft seemed to be bobbing up and down in unison with the continuous throbbing of the ship's engines. Darkness fell, and I joined in a game of cards in the dimly-lit hold of the ship, taking a swig now and again from my last bottle of pale ale.

After a couple of hours we were really being tossed about in the choppy sea, and some of the lads succumbed to the relentless, violent, up-down-and-sideways movements of the craft. The card schools broke up as one after another the lads dropped out, retching into their sick bags as they sat on the floor with their backs up against the sides of the tethered tanks. One of them was laid out flat on a tank's steel engine cover, his face looking a bit green, and moaning in great discomfort.

There must have been a sea dog amongst my ancestors, though, as I didn't feel any effect whatsoever. Instead, I looked round at the recumbent forms of my fellow tank crew, reflecting that men who had been strangers just a few months before were now close colleagues, and were about to share with me in fighting our way over the Normandy beaches.

A troop of Churchills contained three tanks, each tank having five crew members. The troop commander was normally a

2

commissioned officer, and acted as tank commander for the leading tank; the second tank was commanded by the troop sergeant; and the third by the troop corporal.

My tank was number two in our troop, and our tank commander and troop sergeant was Frank Ellis. He was a married man, aged about 28, with fair hair and a stocky physique. Originally from Bolton, Frank had a jovial personality and was much given to breaking out into song - a habit which rapidly led us to nickname him Frank Sinatra.

Lying on the deck alongside Sergeant Ellis was our tank driver, Joe Whelan, a dark-haired Liverpudlian of medium height and build. Joe must have been about 25 at the time, and was a real Scouse character - very witty, with a permanent smile on his face that only disappeared if something upset him. Like myself, he was both single and a Roman Catholic.

Next came Owen Vaughan, our co-driver and hull gunner. Owen was 25 as well, and had fair hair, thin features and a wiry body. He came from Chester, and was a taciturn sort of character who could be very stubborn if you didn't agree with his views or things didn't go the way he wanted, but he was also quite convivial. Owen tended to be a little argumentative at times, which perhaps explained why he was still single.

The crew was completed by our turret gunner, Ion Evans, a short and rather tubby Welshman who must have been about 28. He was a typical Welshman from the valleys, with a rapid singing accent and a habit of ending his sentences with 'look you, boyo', so we unsurprisingly christened him Taffy. He was a married man, and his plump round face would beam at you as he held forth on his favourite topic of conversation - his home in the Rhondda valley.

Studying the dozing faces of my friends and crewmates as we pitched and tossed our way uncomfortably across the Channel, my mind went back to when I first met them, and the arduous months we had spent training in preparation for our present task.

Chapter 2

Preparing for Battle

As a result of the aptitude tests taken while we were with the Royal West Kent Regiment, Tom and I were posted to 57 Training Regiment RAC at Catterick Camp in December 1942 to train as Churchill tank crews. During basic training I was promoted to lance corporal, and eventually passed out as a driver/wireless operator; while Tom became a driver/gunner. We then waited for transfer to a tank regiment, and were overjoyed when we heard we would be returning to the green fields of Kent: on Friday 16 July 1943 we were to go to 151 Regiment RAC in Canterbury.

Travelling on individual postings was always rather irksome, especially on a hot summer's day, and we had to hang about at the railway station loaded up with full pack, haversack, gas mask, helmet, rifle, holstered revolver, and kit bag. But the train arrived at last and we were on our way, down to London and rolling through the Kent countryside with its familiar landmarks.

Fields full of hops, giving off a slight whiff as the young vines began to grow. Apple orchards, with the seemingly sweet smell of the heavily-cropped trees. Fields of grain and vegetables. Dairy farms, with large herds of grazing cows and the occasional bull. Flocks of sheep. Each scene had its individual smell, vying with the stench of the steam engine chugging away up front for a place in the nostrils. Perhaps the smells were imaginary, the sight alone conjuring up the odours for each passing scenario, but 'the garden of England' was here in reality. The train was hot, sticky and crowded, but Kent pulled us like a magnet.

Canterbury arrived with a last squeal of brakes and a noisy

release of steam from the engine's boiler. We donned all our equipment once again: kitbags slung over our shoulders and rifles carried in the hand as we made our way out of the station. Then we dropped everything while we waited for transport to arrive: kitbags on the pavement and rifles propped against the wall. We were soon approached by a cheerful-looking lad in denim battledress, with a black beret pulled down over his right ear.

'Are you the two down from Catterick Camp?'

'Right first time.'

'You're the Dyson twins, then,' as his face lit up with an even bigger smile. 'You don't look alike, though,' he went on, giving us both close scrutiny. 'Perhaps it's your moustache that makes the difference,' he said to me.

'How did you know we were twins, then?' broke in Tom. 'Well, Bill Powland saw the letter from RHQ to our CO saying you were twins and had to serve in the same unit.'

'Oh,' said Tom. 'Who's this Bill Powland?'

'He's the corporal in the squadron office,' replied the driver. 'I'm Bill Hollowbread.'

We drove out of Canterbury along Stone Street, the site of an old Roman road, with Bill putting his foot down hard as if to make up for lost time. Eventually we came to an opening between the hedges, where a board with a legend painted on it showed what I took to be the regimental sign. We drove slowly down the lane and into the forecourt of a large building, in the style of an old manor house. Bill led us to the squadron office, where we were duly documented and told to report again on Monday.

Next stop was our assigned hut, where Bill waited for us to unload our baggage and then abandoned us with a cheery farewell. The hut was empty, but two vacant beds were clearly intended for Tom and me, so we unpacked and organized ourselves. Other residents began to drift in and make our acquaintance: the news that twins were being drafted had obviously preceded us, and I could tell by the inquisitive looks that we were being weighed up for similarity and comparability. I think we were something of a let-down, as they had evidently been expecting identical twins, but they were nevertheless a nice bunch of lads and welcomed us into the fold with enthusiasm.

Over the weekend we explored the place and, to our delight and amazement, were shown a fair-sized swimming pool in the grounds of the mansion. It was a boon during the summer months, and the more hardy lads used it until late autumn.

Tom and I reported to the squadron office on Monday morning and had our first glimpse of Squadron Sergeant-Major Braybrook. We were shown into his office by the orderly sergeant, and left standing to attention at his desk while he tidied some papers into a tray. I guessed him to be in his mid-thirties.

'Stand easy,' he ordered at last. 'So you're the twins. I expected you to be as alike as two peas in a pod.' He managed a little smile, and gazed from one of us to the other quizzically. 'You'll find me fair but firm, and my door is always open for any complaints,' he said, and proceeded to give us a little pep talk on discipline and behaviour. Standards in B Squadron under Sergeant-Major Braybrook were, he assured us, considered to be the best in the regiment.

Next on the agenda was an interview with Captain Cockcroft. I was marched in first, and it soon became evident why, as he opened by saying, 'Let's get the bad news out of the way first, shall we, corporal.' I wondered what was coming next.

'You'll have to take that stripe off. The squadron's already got its full complement of NCOs, unfortunately for you.'

He picked up one of the AB64 Soldiers' Service and Pay Books on his desk and studied it, while I took stock of him. He looked quite youthful - not much older than myself - clean shaven, and fair-haired.

'Here we are, then,' as he turned the pages and wrote on one. 'It's on the record. Reverts to trooper, with effect from 19 July.' Thanks very much, I thought, as he returned the AB64 Part 1 to me. My hard-earned stripe gone for a burton.

'Sorry about that. Now I'll have in Dyson Part 2,' he said, rising from his chair with a little chuckle. I smiled at the joke as he went to open the door, and Tom was duly marched in.

'Oh,' said the captain, looking at us. 'You're fraternal twins.

That makes things a little less complicated for us.' He studied Tom's AB64. 'I see you reverted from lance corporal to trooper when you joined 57th Training Regiment at Catterick. Your brother has had to do the same today, so you're both starting here from scratch. You've both got excellent training reports, so there's no reason why you shouldn't regain promotion if you continue to work hard at it.'

He questioned us about our previous army experience and civilian background, and the talk developed into a conversation rather than our responses being confined to 'Yes, sir'. I detected an amused expression coming over his face as he listened to us, and he finally sat back in his chair with a chuckle. 'I could listen to you two all day. You've got such lovely Cockney accents!' Tom and I just grinned at him.

'Well, before you go, here's a bit of advice for what it's worth. You're obviously very close to each other, and want to be together. Do consider, though, if you really want to go into battle in the same tank. If there's a brew up, one pop and you're both gone.'

We promised to bear his advice in mind, and he dismissed us.

'He's a cheerful charlie,' said Tom as we left. 'Pop, and you're both gone!'

'He's got a point, though, hasn't he?' I replied.

'But he seems a smashing bloke, all the same,' countered Tom, and I nodded in total agreement. On the way out we passed Squadron Sergeant-Major Braybrook (nicknamed, we discovered, Donk; presumably derived from the first part of his name and a reference to the braying of a donkey), and he shouted out, 'Get that stripe off quickly, lad. You're a trooper now.'

We changed into denims, and with the stripes removed from my sleeves I was just like Tom, on the bottom rung of the squadron strength. Our next appointment was with our designated troop in the tank park, for a session on maintenance. As we were B Squadron, all the tanks had names beginning with the letter B. I joined the crew of *Buzzard*, while Tom went to *Briton*. For the time being we were 'spare crews', which every squadron had for obvious reasons.

7

Tom and I settled in quite well with the lads in the squadron, who were predominantly Lancastrians, with the odd few Welsh, Scottish and Irish. The one lone Cockney, named George 'Punchy' Porter, was delighted to be joined by two more from the East End. He was a fair-haired, jolly lad, with a somewhat accentuated Roman nose - hence the nickname. During our first few weeks we managed to gather a new circle of friends around us, not least because we found a way to be the centre of attention.

Our group included Corporal Bill Powland, a semi-professional tenor singer, Tommy Reilly, who played the guitar, and Jock Gould, a trumpet player. The Welfare Officer learned there was the nucleus of a dance band within the ranks (Bill fed him the information), but that one musician was without his instrument: Steve Dyson's violin was at his home in London. The officer, always on the lookout for ways of alleviating the boring life at Stone Street, took the bait.

There was a very large hall at the manor, with parquet flooring suitable for dancing. The officer would beg, borrow or commandeer a piano; send the violinist home to collect his instrument; and rehearse the band to play for ballroom dancing. Service girls could be bussed in to join village girls and Land Army amazons in providing dancing partners (and who knows what else, after the last waltz) for the troops. If the venture proved successful, it would be a real feather in his cap.

On 9 August I was duly summoned by the Welfare Officer. 'Ah, there you are, Dyson. I understand that you play the violin and have experience of playing in a dance band, and your twin brother can play the piano.'

'Yes, sir, that's right. But we only do it for pocket money, really.'

'Well, I've got the idea of forming our own dance band, and if you two would like to get together with the other instrumentalists I'm sure you could knit together a reasonable band. The only snag is your violin still being in London, so I'll arrange for you to have a 48-hour pass to go home this weekend and collect it. How would that suit you?'

After I'd expressed my thanks he continued, 'I'll be putting

Corporal Powland in charge of the project, just to keep you in order. I'm sure he'd like to join you in some of the vocals.' I smiled, as it had been Bill's idea to form a band in the first place.

I got plenty of good-natured banter from the lads when I told them about my luck in getting a pass. Jock bewailed not having left his trumpet back in Scotland, but Tom was philosophical, although naturally disappointed not to be going with me. 'I couldn't very well go home and bring back my piano!'

When I returned with my violin, the band had a few practice sessions and began to get things together satisfactorily. We named ourselves the Squadron Airs (not to be confused with the famous Squadronaires, led by Jimmy Miller), and played to a full house at the first dance on Saturday 21 August. Our programme started with a quickstep tune, 'That's a Plenty', ended with 'Who's Taking You Home Tonight' as the last waltz, and included a few vocals by Bill Powland. It all went down very well, and the happy atmosphere was beneficial to the morale of the troops in our otherwise isolated spot at Stone Street. The isolation did mean, though, that amorous couples among the dancers could disappear easily into the woods around the camp - where, no doubt, more than morale was raised in some cases.

The members of the band also benefited from the arrangement: somehow, we seldom did any fatigues or guard duties. On the disciplinary side, polishing the parquet flooring was added to the list of punishments for wayward lads doing 'jankers'. A few clodhoppers not changing into civvy shoes could make quite a mess of the floor surface with their army boots, and it needed plenty of elbow grease to obliterate the marks and repolish the floor. And with the first dance being such a success, many more were planned.

In the meantime, we were finding a big difference between tank training at Catterick and at Stone Street - mainly in the rules governing reaching the objective. Whereas at Catterick tanks were restricted to roads or open moorland, we were now under simulated battle conditions and had to drive from the start line to the objective as the crow flies. But crows can soar through the air; tanks, having not yet developed wings, are limited to terra

9

firma and have to plough across country regardless. Forty-ton monsters with huge caterpillar tracks were driven roughshod through fields of vegetables and grain, deviating only to skirt round barns and other buildings.

I took part in my first exercise as a tank wireless operator and felt overawed when I looked back at the end of the attack and saw with horror the desecration of the crops behind us. Here we were, amidst all the food shortages, belt tightening, and exhortations to the people to 'dig for victory', crushing and ruining the stuff with reckless abandon under our steel tracks.

As our tank commander left the turret to join in tactical discussions up front, I turned to Ken Rowe, the gunner, and remarked, 'Pity the poor bloody farmers.' I expected him to show sympathy for the sacrilege we had perpetrated, as he was what the big city lads called a 'swede basher' from the little village of Swaffham in Norfolk, but he seemed quite unperturbed. He just gazed at the devastation outlined by the tank tracks, going far back into the distance, and said, 'Don't 'ee cry for the farmers. They be always a'moaning 'bout doing bad, same as publicans. They do alroit - they be gettin' twoice as much back from the government as it's worth.' I didn't probe into his grudge against farmers and pub landlords, but simply retorted, 'Well, the only time I'll enjoy doing this is when we get to Germany. I bet their farmers won't get any compensation from Hitler!'

Tom and I managed to get our privilege leave together, and went home on Friday 17 September. We were sitting in our local pub later on, discussing the inevitability of a cross-Channel invasion, when suddenly some over-ripe tomatoes came whizzing through the air and landed with a splat on the mirror at the far end of the saloon bar, leaving juice dribbling down the Truman's Fine Ales and Stout signwriting on the glass. I turned towards the door just in time to see two young boys dashing away, with a man in hot pursuit. The boys must have escaped through the street market crowd, because the man returned, swearing loudly, and announced, 'It's those bleeding Kray twins.' In later years, of course, their notoriety spread much further afield!

Jock Gould and Tommy Reilly had also managed to get

weekend passes, and came to a party at our house on Saturday night to meet the family. Phyllis and Eileen invited two American soldiers whom they had met when playing with the BeeGees Concert Party at a base in Suffolk, so we were quite a crowd. The Yanks, who said they were 'having a ball', came laden with whisky, cigarettes and cigars, which we all helped to consume; while Tommy brought his guitar and charmed the company with his playing and singing.

Back at Stone Street once more, we resumed advanced tank training with innumerable tactical attacks on targets in the nearby Stelling Minnis area. Our favourite target on these forays was the local windmill. We were also taught the art of camouflaging the tank with string netting and foliage, to blend in with the surroundings and give us an element of surprise.

Sooner or later, most turret crew members experience the agony of a turret hatch lid crashing down on an arm, hand or finger, and I had a painful initiation shortly after returning from leave. The heavy metal lids were held in an upright position by a groove in the strong spring-retaining catch. I dislodged this catch accidentally, and the lid slammed down over the top knuckle joint of my left index finger. The scar it left is still visible today.

Another scar acquired at Stone Street was slightly more inglorious. After a night on the booze we would sometimes go for a swim in the pool, in the belief that the cold water would help to sober us up. One moonlit night in October we decided on a dip, and I was first out after changing. I ran along the edge of the pool and plunged forward in a belly dive, only to see stars as my chin hit the concrete bottom of the pool. Unbeknown to us, the pool had been drained and cleaned that very day, so I landed in about six inches of water left at the bottom. Very dazed, and with blood from my cut chin streaming down to stain the water, I was hauled off to our hut for first aid.

Everybody except me found the whole escapade hilarious, and the following day news of my mishap was all over the camp. Quips came fast and furious: you wanna take more water with it, Steve; fancy a dip in the concrete; who pulled the plug out, Steve? One budding Poet Laureate even pinned a masterpiece on to the squadron noticeboard, which I retrieved for posterity:

> By the light of the silvery moon,
> Steve Dyson dived in the pool.
> Alas there was no water therein,
> My, did he feel a fool.
> The moral there is quite plain to see,
> For those who will swim before sleep.
> It must be the old proverb, of course:
> Look before you leap.

The weeks passed, and as we approached the end of the very muddy autumn season our squadron attained a high standard of preparation for tank warfare. We were much assisted in our efforts by our officers, who were a smashing lot and won the respect of us all with the way they mucked in with the lads during exercises.

The only exception was one major, a dapper and supercilious-looking chap, the image of a regular army officer with his military bearing, thin black moustache and closely clipped black hair. His manner was abrasive, and he was given to berating junior officers within earshot of the troopers. I thought he must have been weaned at Sandhurst, straight from public school, and was amazed to be told that he had been a bus driver back in civvies. Even then, the tale seemed so unlikely that I didn't wholly believe it until I saw the verification in print, long after the war ended.

By now we were individually and collectively ready to face the tasks allotted to our regiment in the impending cross-Channel invasion. We'd done exercises with the infantry, and reached a good understanding of how best to co-operate under their command in battle, supporting them in both attack and defence. In this support role we differed from the lighter and faster tanks in the armoured divisions, whose task was to exploit the holes punched in enemy lines by artillery/infantry/tank attacks, and pour through the gaps in large numbers.

Our squadron had also already received some of the new Mark VI Churchill tanks, modified and fitted with a 75mm gun to replace the six-pounder gun tanks, as the first stage in re-equipping the whole regiment with the new tanks. The 75mm gun could fire high explosive shells as well as solid armour-piercing shells, whereas at that time the six-pounders could only fire AP shells. AP was excellent when engaging and shooting at single targets, like another tank or a self-propelled gun; but for wider-spread targets, such as anti-tank gun posts, machine-gun nests or buildings occupied by the enemy, HE was much more effective, and thus a useful addition to our armoury.

As if in recognition of our battle-ready status, in December 1943 151 RAC's title was changed to 107 Regiment RAC (The King's Own). We also moved into winter quarters.

Tom and I could hardly believe our new location: Shornecliff Barracks, Cheriton, Folkestone. We'd come full circle, as we'd left the same barracks to begin our tank training in 1942. The lads were pleased to find we'd been stationed there before, on the grounds that we would know the layout and could show them the town and the best places for entertainment. 'I'll have to look up a couple of birds I know there, and I don't mean seagulls,' I said to Jock. He laughed. 'Ye're a wee divil wi' the girls, Steve.'

We marked the end of our stay at Stone Street by visiting the nearby village of Chilham. We'd been there a couple of times previously, during the summer, and found it to be a most delightful 'olde worlde' place: period style houses; a lovely village square, with a castle keep on one side and a beautiful old church on the other; a picturesque, low, timbered pub; and all situated atop a hill. Bill Powland remarked that most of us would probably never see it again, so Tom and I, Jock Gould, Tommy Reilly and Punchy Porter accompanied Bill on a pilgrimage.

The village, of course, looked very different in the winter. Gone were the summer roses and masses of flowers everywhere; but this seemed only to highlight its winter beauty. Red creepers climbing around the buildings. Evergreen trees and shrubs. Odd brown leaves still clinging here and there on the branches of deciduous trees. We strolled around the castle grounds, then returned to the village just as the pubs were opening. We were soon supping our pints in front of a blazing fire in the public bar of the White Horse, in the village square.

Somehow the warmth of the fire, the cosiness of the pub and the friendliness of the locals made our visit well worthwhile. We sat there, drinking and chatting away on all sorts of topics, with some agreeing, some disagreeing. The scenario embodied the living proof of the freedoms we took for granted, and which the country was fighting to retain. The freedom of speech. The freedom to go anywhere, at any time. The freedom to choose our own way of life. The freedoms bestowed by democracy.

We left the peace and tranquillity of this rural countryside soon afterwards to take up residence in Cheriton Barracks on the outskirts of Folkestone. We were looking forward to living in comparative comfort after the austere conditions at Stone Street: it had proved to be quite reasonable and enjoyable as a summer camp; but in the bleak winter months it was far from that. We also needed a change – Tom and I had been at Stone Street for five months, most of the others for even longer, and nobody relished the thought of spending Christmas there.

The tanks moved off in convoy down the road, passing our favourite old target windmill at Stelling Minnis in the distance as we did so. It was as if the regiment was giving it a final salute in honour of the part it had played in our training, with a grand parade as the convoy of tanks rumbled on.

It didn't take long to travel the 15 miles to our destination – where, to my surprise, we carried on down a side lane instead of turning up to the barracks. At the far end of the lane we parked our tanks under the trees lining the road, and I wondered why we hadn't parked in the barracks themselves. Not until much later did I realize that concentrating our tanks in this area may have been part of the subterfuge to fool the Germans, so they would believe that the invasion, when it came, would be in the Pas de Calais area and across the Strait of Dover. It seemed the obvious choice to most British people anyway; not many would have bet a brass farthing against it at the time, me included.

14

Chapter 3

Waiting for the Second Front

So Tom and I were back once again in familiar surroundings, and showing the lads our favourite Folkestone haunts. We saw more damage from cross-Channel German guns and air raids than when we were last there: it wasn't called 'Hell Fire Corner' for nothing. But, ignoring the intermittent artillery fire, of which we were given no warning in any case, and the occasional air raid alert, life was pleasant enough. We settled into an easy routine, with evenings and weekends free, beyond occasional security duties in barracks and on the tank harbour.

Apart from a wide choice of pubs, there were cinemas, dance halls, and, of course, plenty of girls - the icing on the cake for lads who desired female company, and most of them did. Not only were there local girls, but also an influx of service girls from surrounding areas. There was no doubt about what many of them were seeking, apart from the entertainment facilities in the town: they seemed to become more liberal with their favours the nearer the 'second front' appeared to be. Make the most of it while you can!

Tom and I did just that in another context: Folkestone's direct rail link to London proved too much of a temptation, and it was easy to nip off at the weekend unless you were down for a duty. It was risky, of course, but we and a few other fellow Cockneys in the squadron were willing to take the chance. We were lucky that not one of us was apprehended for being AWOL during this period. I feel sure our own officers knew what was going on, but did the Nelson act and turned a blind eye.

Tom and I went home for a nine-day leave on Thursday 30 December. We'd been hoping to get back for Christmas, but had no luck - perhaps our role in helping with the squadron entertainment had something to do with it. Scotsmen Jock Gould and Tommy Reilly could have had Christmas leave, but put it off to allow them to be home for Hogmanay. They came to London with us and stayed overnight, travelling on to Scotland on the Friday; then reversed the procedure when they returned a week later. On this second visit they came armed with a haggis for Mum, which provoked much merriment. In the meantime Tom and I saw the New Year in with the family, with a marvellous party at home. We all rejoined our unit on Saturday 8 January 1944.

I detected a note of cautious optimism among the people in the East End during our leave, even though they continued to suffer hardships. Shortages of most things were still commonplace; even coal for the little open fires around which families huddled in the cold winter days was scarce. There were still sneak air raids and constant alerts. But there seemed to be a feeling of hope now, helping to offset the miserable adversities of the fifth wartime Christmas and New Year. Many people believed the war would be over by next Christmas, and this thought alone cheered them up and enabled them to endure the discomforts.

During the early part of the year, London's West End was bursting at the seams with British and foreign troops; the latter predominantly American. The Piccadilly 'floozies' had never had it so good - business was booming, thanks to the build-up of forces in the south in preparation for the coming invasion. I could detect an air of expectancy on all sides: London had been battered, and was still beset by 'scalded cat' raids and constant alerts, kept awake by terrific artillery and rocket anti-aircraft fire. But Londoners braved the falling shrapnel as determinedly as they went about their business, with more of a spring in their steps nowadays. All the sacrifices of the past few years would soon be proved to have been worthwhile.

The British people knew that an invasion by the Allies, somewhere on the French coast, was inevitable if we were to gain

1. Private Steve Dyson, East Surrey Regiment, 1940.

2. B Squadron, 107 Regiment RAC, Germany, 1945. *Top:* Jock Gould,
Steve Dyson; *Middle:* George Metcalf, Bill Blewett; *Standing:* Captain
Mike Hill, Bob Garbutt, ?, Sergeant Bradley.

a quick and decisive victory. The Allied landing at Anzio at the end of January was a sideshow, despite the fierce German opposition. It could be a prolonged and drawn-out affair, even stalemate, if we had to rely on the Russians advancing from the east and the western Allies slogging their way up from Italy in the south to achieve victory. There was some satisfaction in the heavy and sustained bombing campaign against Berlin and other big German towns and cities; but bombing civilians and industrial targets alone wouldn't finish the war - an invasion was needed. Many people voiced the opinion that it would be a blood-bath, but were nevertheless prepared to make the sacrifice now rather than prolong the agony.

The people of Folkestone shared this view, particularly since cross-Channel shelling was a constant threat to the town's population and played heavily on their nerves. They suffered many casualties and much damage to property, which they bore with commendable fortitude. Only a successful invasion could stop it.

I experienced my first 'near miss' while we were carrying out maintenance on the tank a few days after we arrived. Bob Garbutt and I were changing a track plate when suddenly there was a loud explosion, followed by a shower of earth descending on us. Bob looked up, startled and mystified, and dived under the tank. Then, as though realising the immediate danger had passed, he poked his head out and shouted, 'What the bloody hell was that?'

'That,' I said, with an air of one who'd had previous experience under fire in Folkestone, 'was a German shell.' Fortunately it had landed in a field about 50 yards away from us. Our crew clambered on top of the tank, as did the adjacent crews, and surveyed the crater left in the earth nearby, with a wisp of smoke still visible. We all agreed it was too close for comfort and, by some coincidence, within minutes all the crews on the park suddenly found jobs to do inside their tanks for a while.

My only other close one happened one evening a few days after Tom and I returned from leave. We were on a pub crawl in the town centre with the two Jocks, Punchy and Bill Powland, and left one pub to go to another in the main high street. As we reached the corner we heard the now familiar loud explosion of the missile

17

on impact, its echo reverberating through the still night air, followed by the crash of masonry and broken glass. We stopped in our tracks and crouched down by the side of a building for protection: the shell could only have landed a few yards away, because the air was full of bits and pieces forming a dust cloud.

Recovering from the sudden shock, we went round the corner into the high street and discovered how close it was - two shops down, the front was completely demolished. It was fortunate that it happened at night rather than in the daytime, when shoppers were about. Within minutes the fire service arrived to deal with a fire resulting from the explosion. We didn't dally there long in the dust and smoke, but brushed our clothes down and went to the next pub to drink a toast to our lucky escape.

After the winter hibernation, which was devoted to getting our tanks into tip-top condition, we moved out of barracks. We almost retraced our steps, or I should say tracks, as we moved back into the rural area around Canterbury, to a village with the happy-sounding name of Goodnestone. We came to rest in Fredville Park, a little way out of the village. After parking our tanks in concrete bays on the side of the road leading through the woods, we settled ourselves into Nissen hut quarters. It was a lovely day, and the countryside was just beginning to come alive with the first signs of spring.

It was quite clear that the regiment was under orders to get everything, and every man, into battle-ready condition. Some fresh faces arrived, with battle experience in North Africa and Italy, to pass on the knowledge acquired in previous tank warfare actions to us novices. We put this into practice in a further series of exercises, and derived great benefit from their expertise.

I was privileged to see Monty one day, on one of his morale-boosting trips to the major units involved in the invasion build-up. Thousands of us, from various units, were assembled in a large field before his arrival. When he ascended the platform, a deathly hush came over the waiting throng - you could sense the air of expectancy on all sides to hear the great man speak. One awed voice behind me spoke for us all as he murmured, 'It's like the coming of the Messiah.'

The general addressed us over a microphone, his voice coming out loud and clear through speakers rigged up around the perimeter of the field. There was no doubt of his magnetism as he held the audience spellbound, with his message coming over in his inimitable, clipped rhetoric. 'We are going to invade Western Europe with the greatest armada ever assembled, and with a huge superiority in the air. We are going to knock the Hun for six! You and I are part of a great team, assembled by the Allies, that will deal a deadly blow to Hitler and all he stands for.'

It was a great morale-booster: we loved the cricket analogy, and he had every man solidly behind him. Everyone was left feeling he had a vital part to play in the crusade. As Monty finished his speech by wishing us luck in the coming battles, a spontaneous burst of cheers from the congregation drowned the drone of a flight of bombers on their way to drop their loads somewhere in Europe. Monty smiled to acknowledge the acclaim, looked up at the aircraft, and quipped, 'It's all right, they're ours.' This well-known phrase, which had on occasions been inaccurate, had the lads rolling in the aisles. With a final wave he descended from the platform and was whisked away in a staff car, no doubt on his way to another venue to give a repeat performance.

Since we arrived at Goodnestone, everyone due for leave had been given 12 days in lieu of the normal seven. We didn't take this as benevolence on the part of the army brass, but reasoned it must be because it would be our last leave in this country – and the last leave ever for the unlucky ones who would never return from the other side. We had to make the most of it.

Tom and I, Punchy and the two Jocks went on our leave on Friday 31 March. Punchy managed, at short notice, to rearrange the date of his leave to coincide with ours, and travelled up to London with us. We had two weekends, so the Jocks stayed at our home over the first one before going on to Scotland.

It was London's 'Salute the Soldier' fund-raising week, and Bethnal Green War Savings Committee (whose chairman was the mayor, a friend of my parents) organised the various activities in our borough. The highlight was to be a Salute the Soldier Revue given by BeeGee Productions Unlimited on Saturday 1 April.

Eileen had obtained tickets for Tom and me, the two Jocks and Punchy, but we were unprepared for what happened when we arrived at the hall: we were given VIP treatment, with reserved seats in the front row alongside the mayor, mayoress, and other councillors. We soon realised this was stage-managed to give the utmost impact and swell the collection boxes that evening – a sentimental ingredient to loosen the purse strings.

The government had just announced that coastal and fringe areas on the Channel facing France were to be prohibited zones, with the exception of people living there. Police, and their military counterparts, would check the identity of all travellers to these areas. The new regulation brought home to people that the long-awaited second front in Europe was now imminent; and the compère of the show played on this to arouse the emotions of the audience. He welcomed the members of the forces amongst the audience, and especially the five tank crew from the same squadron, sitting there in the front row, who no doubt would soon be in the spearhead of the invasion. This brought loud applause, and one could clearly hear the jingle of coins dropping in collection boxes. It was a little embarrassing, I must confess, but as it was in a good cause I forgave Eileen for conspiring with the show organisers to boost their takings in this way.

I still have the souvenir programme, price threepence, and it brings back memories of a show that was almost up to professional standards, even though all the company were Civil Defence volunteers. The sketches, not unnaturally, were skits about soldiers and their wives or sweethearts, sergeant-majors and officers, and so forth. The programme states: 'In the event of an Air Raid Warning being received, it will be announced from the stage', but fortunately the proceedings were uninterrupted.

The two Jocks and Punchy were loud in their praise of the cast, and very impressed with the versatility shown by my sisters, of whom I was justly proud. After the show we had a party with some of the cast at our home, but the big party (the last one before who-knows-what) was saved for the end of the week.

We had to make the most of this last leave, so we crammed as much in as possible. Jock and Tommy left for Scotland, while Punchy, Tom and I paid a few visits to the West End. It was very different from our last leave, with a dramatic decrease in the numbers of service men and women in the area. Previously you could hardly move a few yards without seeing an American; now they were few and far between. Traders, publicans and the entertainment industry were beginning to feel the pinch, and would miss the free-spending Americans most of all.

It was also a devastating blow for the prostitutes, who now had to vie with each other amid intense competition to attract customers. After being accosted several times as we walked from Piccadilly Circus to Soho, I commented, 'I wouldn't be surprised if they put up 'sale' notices, and paraded with sandwich boards advertising their prices.'

'I wouldn't go with one of them even if they paid me,' replied Punchy, and Tom and I concurred with his sentiments. The average man 'wouldn't touch them with a barge pole', feeling it abhorrent that a woman should sell her body. But conversely, the same type of man would have no scruples in accepting 'favours' freely given by a woman.

Wherever one went in London the air was full of speculation about the second front. Everyone had their own ideas of date and venue, and some were even putting their money on it in local pub or workplace sweepstakes. It was second front fever, and everybody was caught up in it. But they all shared one belief: the Channel would run red with blood. Not very comforting for those of us who would be taking part!

At the end of our leave, on Wednesday 12 April, we said goodbye to everyone before catching an early evening train back to Goodnestone. The atmosphere was charged with emotion; a mixture of tears and laughter, as we cracked a few jokes while making our farewells. At the back of everybody's mind, of course, was all the talk about the coming blood-bath, in which Tom and I would soon participate. So it was hugs and kisses from the girls, a handshake from Dad, and a few tears rolling down Mum's cheeks, which she quickly brushed away with her handkerchief. Then we were down the stairs and away on our journey. My inner

21

feelings were similar to those I felt when I left to join the army way back in 1940: uncertainty at what lay ahead.

Back at camp we found things had been moving along fast while we'd been away. The regiment was now on a war footing and in battle-ready condition. All leave was ended, and everybody was confined to the Goodnestone district. Rumours were rife about our role in the invasion; although, to the relief of everyone except the death-or-glory element in some of the officers, we knew our tanks wouldn't be used in the initial assault on the beaches.

This near-suicidal role, or so it seemed to most of our lads, would be performed by tanks specially adapted for that type of operation: duplex drive amphibious Shermans. They were designed to be launched from ships at sea, with flotation collars keeping them buoyant as they were driven across the water to the beach. Once there, they would give covering fire to the invading infantry as they waded ashore and advanced through the hail of lead coming from enemy positions.

There was also the Sherman Crab tank, whose role was to explode mines in its path by flailing the ground with revolving chains. These tanks would be put ashore from tank landing craft, and their guns would add to our firepower against enemy strongpoints.

Then there were specially adapted Churchill tanks with a Petard mortar mounted in the turret, which fired a missile of tremendous explosive power and could engage a concrete pillbox at 200-300 feet, putting it out of action by cracking it open. These Churchill tanks of the AVREs (Assault Vehicle Royal Engineers) had other useful equipment enabling them to cross anti-tank ditches and soft ground. They could carry fascines - huge bundles of wood held together with wire - which would be dumped in anti-tank ditches to help cross the void; bridging ramps; and a roll of road bedding to assist armoured vehicles negotiating the soft ground ashore. The Churchills would be landed on the beaches by LCTs.

Another adapted Churchill was the Crocodile flamethrower, which could eject an awesome stream of fire up to about a hundred yards away. It had a flame gun fitted in place of the machine gun in the hull. A trailer towed at the rear of the Crocodile contained the jelly-like fuel. The fire would stick to, and burn, anything in its path. The Crocodiles would also be put ashore by LCTs once the beach was secured.

We had seen all these specialised tanks, and experienced their capabilities in action, during realistic exercises on previous manoeuvres. I well remember the time we first set eyes on the peculiar contraptions, while we were stationed at Stone Street. The day before the visit our troop leader announced that we were to see 'Hobart's Funnies'. The lads immediately thought we were going to a show by that name. Not so: it was a demonstration of the various specially designed tanks to be used for a seaborne invasion. Most of them, we learned, were the products of an inventive genius called Major-General Hobart. Our reaction on seeing them, as with most troops who saw them for the first time, was that they were funny-looking tanks; hence the nickname Hobart's Funnies.

Our own 34 Tank Brigade Churchills were to be used in a different role from that of the Funnies. Once a secure beachhead had been achieved 'somewhere over there', we would be landed on the beaches from LCTs to take on enemy armour thrown into the battle in an attempt to destroy Allied forces and push them back into the sea. Our job was not only to blunt these desperate attacks but, in co-operation with infantry and artillery on land and the big guns of offshore battleships, to force a breach in the enemy line for the fast tanks of the armoured divisions to pour through. The RAF, meanwhile, would take its toll of enemy reinforcements en route to the battlefront by road and rail.

We were briefed on the part we had to play, but only the planners knew where and when it would take place. We had one last preparation to make: sealing up and waterproofing our tanks to enable them to be driven onto the beach, through water if necessary, after disembarking down the ramp of the LCTs. This job was to be completed at our final destination prior to embarkation on the LCTs, and we were moved to the village of Headley, in Hampshire, to carry out the task.

Travelling across country from Kent to Hampshire by train,

with our tanks secured on flat wagons at the rear, was a novelty. We'd moved by rail previously, though, when we fired our 75mm guns at Larkhill ranges on the Wiltshire Downs, so we knew exactly how to secure them to the wagon irons. All went according to plan, and as we passed through Kent, Sussex, Surrey and into Hampshire we could see the massive build-up of invasion forces. Southern England was bursting at the seams, with every available bit of land utilised as temporary camps. Military convoys were here and there on the roads - which may have been the reason for moving us by rail rather than on tank transporters, as we would have added to the road congestion.

Headley was a lovely little place, set in the countryside about three miles each way from Hindhead on the Surrey border to the east and Liphook, on the Hampshire border, to the south. Once established in our billets, we got down to the urgent task of waterproofing the tanks. It was an intricate and technical job, requiring a lot of painstaking work, and one that no one would dare bodge, as there was too much at stake. Each crew was responsible for the work on their own tank. There were the inevitable, sometimes heated, discussions on the right way to do things after reading the instructions issued with the kit, but in the end problems were solved amicably and satisfactorily.

The tanks had to be able to operate in water to a depth of five feet, so extension ducts were fitted to the air inlet vents on either side of the hull, and long extension pipes to the exhaust system. Rivets and bolts were cleaned and painted with waterproof paint, while inspection covers and all areas where water could penetrate were sealed with a rubber compound. Balloon fabric was glued around the ring of the turret, gun mountings and driver's visor, under which ran a continuous length of cordtex. When detonated from a switch in the driver's compartment, this exploded and blew all the fabric off, so the tank could go into immediate action if necessary.

We enjoyed the work, as it was something entirely different from the usual routine, and there wasn't much else to do in camp apart from guard duty. To thwart any boredom, however, the officers organised some inter-troop competitions, into which we entered with great gusto. By the end of May, when the waterproofing had been completed, our tanks had begun to look like Hobart's Funnies, and we had nothing to do but hang about waiting for the starting pistol.

Headley had one thing going for it that Goodnestone did not: a lovely big pub called the Crown, which stood in a strategically accessible position more or less on our doorstep. Needless to say, it was well patronised by our lads, in addition to some of the Canadian forces stationed thereabouts. Other than isolated bits of friction generated by loud-mouthed 'Canuks' up to their eyeballs in booze, we generally got on well with them; although their vernacular on some things had a different connotation to ours, which led to misunderstandings at times.

On one occasion I was standing at the bar with some of the lads when a Canuk sidled up to me and said, 'Have you got a rubber, buddy?' Assuming he wanted an eraser, I answered in the negative, but told him to ask the barmaid for one. He looked at me in consternation, then explained what he wanted in greater detail - a condom! As with our American cousins, their bum was a tramp, whereas our bum was something we sat on; their elevator was our lift; and so it went on.

Early one crisp April morning, Tom and I were on ground patrol duty and reached the fence separating the Crown's garden from our camp. We loitered there, observing some of our planes winging their way over in the direction of Europe. 'Another delivery of belated Easter eggs for Hitler,' I said. We turned to resume our patrol, when Tom suddenly noticed a couple of large, blue eggs lying on the grass a few yards the other side of the fence. His eyes popped out like two fried eggs, and he licked his lips in anticipation.

'You're not going to...' I was about to say 'pinch 'em', but he cut me off in mid-sentence.

'No,' he laughed. 'I'm not going to; I'm not going to leave them there.' Calling on the experience of a bit of poaching learned during his days working in a travelling boxing booth, he quickly clambered over the fence at a strategic point where a garden shrub hid the view from the pub. This disturbed some ducks in the shrubbery, which quickly waddled away quacking like fury. Waiting until the noise of the ducks had subsided, Tom poked his head round the shrub and scanned the pub windows to make sure the blackout blinds were all still down before he made his next move. Then he darted out, picked up the eggs, and was back again behind the concealing shrub in the twinkling of an eye. A few moments later he rejoined me, holding his precious booty, and with a self-satisfied look on his face.

'Come on,' he said. 'Let's see if the cookhouse is open yet.'

We were in luck: Jock, the cook, had just arrived. He was a tall, chunkily-built, dark-haired Scot, and seemed to have a permanent smile on his face. He was just about to open the door when he caught sight of us. 'Ye're a wee bit airly for a brew.'

Tom held out the eggs, one in each hand, for Jock's perusal.

'Och mon! Duck eggs. A wee bit strong fe' ye.'

'What about doing something with them for us, then,' said Tom.

'Boiled, fried or poached, mon?' replied Jock, laughing; and shortly afterwards Tom and I were hidden in the storeroom, away from prying eyes, each enjoying a poached egg on toast washed down with a steaming cup of char.

This was the first time I tasted a duck egg, and I did find it very different from chicken eggs and rather strong, as Jock had forecast. It wasn't the first time for Tom, though. He was quite partial to them and for the next few mornings, just after reveille, he disappeared to do a little more poaching.

A few nights later, in the bar of the Crown, we overheard the landlady talking to one of the locals. 'I don't know what's happened to my ducks lately. They've gone off laying. I wonder if it's all this aircraft noise affecting them.' The landlord chimed in: 'Mebbe it's someone getting at 'em. If I catch 'em, they'll get a taste of me twelve bore. Man or beast, I won't care.' Funnily enough, the following day the ducks started laying again, according to a delighted landlady discussing the phenomenon with some locals in the bar that evening. 'I still don't understand it,' she exclaimed. Tom and I exchanged knowing glances, and a wry smile.

Our unit was completely ready, with tanks all waterproofed to land on the beaches and, as Monty put it, knock the Hun for six. We were like dogs straining at the end of a leash and knew the invasion could be any day now.

Chapter 4

D-Day at Last

The day the whole world seemed to be waiting for dawned on 6 June. D-Day.

In the early hours of the morning we learned from a BBC broadcast that the invasion of Normandy had begun. British, American and Canadian troops, under the command of General Eisenhower, had assaulted the beaches at several points. Massed airborne landings had been made behind enemy lines, and all was reported to be going well so far.

The excitement in our camp was intense: the waiting was over, and we could start the countdown for our own D-Day. We gazed, open-mouthed, at the endless fleets of white-striped planes and gliders winging their way over to Normandy. Camp routine almost came to a standstill as we lapped up news broadcasts on the progress of the battles. The evening papers, at one penny each, were the best bargain of the day, if you were lucky enough to obtain one in the stampede to buy them. They made exhilarating reading.

'A massive armada of thousands of ships and thousands of planes has taken part in the assault on Normandy.... Beachheads have been won on Hitler's Atlantic Wall.... Churchill says, "All is going to plan".... The King will broadcast to the nation at 9pm.'

All this was avidly read and digested over and over again. The expected blood-bath, feared by almost everyone, had not materialised - initial assault casualties, although heavy, especially on the American sector, were very much lighter than had been anticipated.

During the next few days we followed the course of the battles on maps of Normandy, newly unwrapped from sealed packages now that D-Day had revealed the secrets of venue and date. Some of our young troop officers were like dogs with two tails in their happiness that the waiting was over. 'Good show, what! We'll be in amongst the Hun soon now, and it can't come too soon!'

Most of the lads were revelling in the excitement of it all, but conscious of how near we were to the time when we would participate in the assault as follow-up forces. We felt it was a job that had to be done, and the sooner we got cracking the better. But we waited, and waited, for the call.

Filling our time as best we could, we were given a briefing by the squadron leader, Major Davies, using a large wall map of Normandy to explain the strategy. The British and Canadians of the Second Army were to draw all available enemy armour to their sector and engage them in a battle of attrition. The Americans, meanwhile, would prepare for a massive thrust out of their sector into the open country. There were wry comments from the lads at this: why couldn't it be the other way round?

The arrival of shoals of rocket-propelled bombs over London during the second half of June was a great worry to those of us with families in the capital. Londoners could take air raids with bombs dropped from conventional planes; but these infernal things, falling from the sky with no warning, were by all accounts more demoralising. Variously described as robot planes, V1s or doodlebugs, they were Hitler's secret weapon, by which he hoped to bring London to its knees.

Although it was a worry for lads from the Smoke, a certain court martial awaited anyone caught AWOL attempting to go and see their families. It was practically impossible, anyway, as we were under tight security in the camp, and railways and roads were subject to stringent checks by military and civil police. We Cockney lads were also under scrutiny from the beady eyes of Donk, SSM Braybrook. It was probably just as well, however, that only a few days after the first doodlebugs were reported to be dropping haphazardly over London the order we were all expecting came through.

Being ordered to move to the embarkation area concentrated our minds on our own destiny rather than the fate of those in danger in London: all was hustle and bustle as we packed up and prepared to leave Headley the following morning. We were to do the journey on our own tracks, so the crews' only job now was to remove the sealing from the drivers' visors so we could take to the road. The visors would eventually be resealed.

We were delighted at the thought of getting moving again, as our tanks had been motionless for too long. I'm sure I speak for all tank men in saying there is some sort of affinity between you and your tank, and I was looking forward to taking my place in the turret of *Buzzard* for my trip to Normandy. It was 'my' tank and, well, I just loved it.

The night before the move was spent saying goodbye to the friends we had made in Headley and the Crown. We finished the evening in the pub, with Tommy Reilly strumming away on his guitar and the lads singing the Great War song, 'Goodbyee, goodbyee, wipe the tears from your eyes, don't cryee'. It was the obvious and spontaneous choice: if this was going to be our last communal booze-up before embarking, it would be one to remember.

We were on the road to the coast at the crack of dawn on Friday 23 June, most of us unsurprisingly nursing hangovers. Mine wore off after a mile or two travelling with head and shoulders sticking out of the turret, the cool morning air blowing into my face and sweeping the cobwebs away as we steadily bowled along in follow-my-leader style. Squadron HQ was at the front of the column, with my troop about halfway down the long line of tanks, and I was kept busy ensuring my radio was on net on HQ frequency. Our tanks looked a funny lot, all sealed up and with the extended exhaust pipes and air louvre ducts sticking up and rattling.

Tom, who was still a spare crew man, was travelling with the motorised echelon at the rear, but it wasn't long before I saw his smiling face again. After about ten miles the column stopped for a short break, which gave time to cool the engines down a bit and warm the tank crews up with a hot cup of char. The cook's truck drove along the line with Tom (who else) helping Jock fill our mugs with the precious brew.

Joe Whelan, the driver of *Buzzard*, looked as if he could do with it more than the other crew members. In follow-my-leader convoys, the further back your vehicle is the harder it is to keep up with those at the head of the column. You have to slow down at times, and at others go like the clappers to keep up. Joe, a jovial Liverpudlian, looked a little strained, but declined the troop leader's suggestion that he hand over to Taffy Evans, our co-driver. The Scouse insisted, in his thick accent, that he was quite OK; after being off the road for a couple of months, he wanted his hands on that tiller bar for as long as possible before landing on the Normandy beaches.

I suppose the inaction at Headley had made us all a little rusty. Even some troop officers were heard speaking to their crews on the A-set net, reserved for speech and morse key communication to squadron HQ or even further. They should have moved the switch on the control box to either the B-set (short range radio for troop communication between the troop leader and the other two tank commanders), or the IC (an intercom allowing the tank commander to talk to the rest of his crew). These human errors were usually met with a sarcastic rebuke from the squadron leader, because it was of the utmost importance to select the correct switch - especially in giving instructions to the driver of a 40-ton monster on the move. There's no point in telling the driver to change direction, or halt, if the switch is on A and he can't hear you. Accidents happen that way, as I knew by experience: the tank I was in one day at Stone Street went straight through a brick wall.

After about an hour, during which we relieved ourselves behind nearby bushes, we received the order to move off. We had chain-smoked and jawed amongst ourselves during the break, marvelling at the vast amounts of vehicles, artillery, tanks and military equipment we'd seen over the last few miles. It was even more concentrated as we moved nearer the coast, and I wondered at the logistic problems of assembling all this in the right order and shipping it over to Normandy.

We eventually reached our pre-embarkation point a few miles

from Portsmouth, at a village by the name of Waterlooville (a good omen, I thought, with Wellington's famous victory), where we went into leaguer and awaited embarkation orders.

Bad storms in the Channel had seriously delayed the Allied build-up on the beachhead, and from 19 - 22 June the Mulberry harbour had been badly knocked about and damaged by the heaviest seas seen in the Channel for many years. There was consequent chaos on the landing beaches, as the CO told us in a general briefing to the assembled squadron the next morning. The storm delays had a knock-on effect, holding up the sailing of units and equipment needed to expand the beachhead; but for the weather, he told us, we would have been on the other side by now. As it was, we could expect another few days' delay before moving to our embarkation point. For some of us, me included, it was rather disappointing: now we'd started we wanted to get on with it, and waiting about was only prolonging the agony.

There was nothing for us to do except mandatory security patrols. Tanks had been refuelled with petrol and oil, ammunition stowed away in the hull racks, and we were all ready to fight directly we landed if necessary. We whiled away the time playing cards, reading, writing letters home, and going for walks in the vicinity of the village – taking a last look, as it were, at the English countryside. It was during one of these walks that Tom and I, and the friends with us, witnessed a harrowing sight which abruptly silenced us and put the collywobbles in our tummies.

We reached a level crossing adjacent to the station, where a Red Cross train was standing and casualties from Normandy were being transferred to a fleet of ambulances to take them on to hospitals. We watched in horror, and complete silence, as a tragic procession of men was led or carried from the train to the ambulances. Stretcher cases; men hobbling along on crutches, some with one or more limbs missing; sightless ones, being individually guided; white bandages, some with red bloodstains seeping through from wounds...

It was a sobering experience for us all, and took the edge off our impatience to rush into battle. For most of these unfortunates, the war was over. For us, the battles were yet to come.

At the back of my mind lurked childhood memories of being taken to see my Uncle Ted (my mother's brother, a regular RSM), who lay in a hospital bed for four years with a broken neck before dying. I thought that I would rather die than be paralysed.

A couple of days later we got the order to move to the Solent for embarkation. We also heard the wonderful news that the Americans had captured Cherbourg, although on the British flank we were still contained in the beachhead. It had developed into a real slogging match, because the bulk of the enemy Panzers had been concentrated in this sector as Monty had anticipated. Attempts to capture Caen had been thwarted, and Monty's plan to take the town in the early stages of the invasion had suffered a setback and was behind schedule. His idea was for the line to hinge on Caen, with the Americans breaking out on the opposite flank; but the hinge needed oiling!

This was the state of play, to use Monty's parlance, when we were sent in to bat. To be historically accurate, the 34th Independent Tank Brigade (comprising 107, 147 and 153 Regiments RAC under the command of Brigadier W. S. Clarke) was now under orders to embark and be transported for deployment in the beachhead. For Tom and I, our personal D-Day had come.

When the order came to mount up ready to move I had one last thing to do, which I hadn't been looking forward to: say goodbye, or, please God, only au revoir, to Tom. He was going with the other spare crews in the squadron echelon sailing with the main bulk of the regiment. At least we would be on separate ships, which reduced the odds of us both going down to Davy Jones's locker.

We spent a few minutes together before the echelon moved off; then, with a strong handshake and a 'see you over there', Tom jumped into the passenger seat of a half-track vehicle and was driven away by Bill Hollowbread. Please God we both make it across, I said to myself, as I waved him off and returned to my troop.

The echelon had been gone about half an hour before we

eventually got the order to move off. I climbed up the tank and into the turret, took my position next to the tank commander, and donned my earphones to listen in to orders. After a few minutes we got the 'off' from our troop commander: we were the last troop away in the convoy.

We drove along the road leading to the coast with many hold-ups on the way. There was so much military traffic about that it was like Piccadilly Circus in the rush hour. Civilians scarcely gave us a second look - it was an everyday occurrence in these parts.

We eventually came to a halt at Fareham, in a road near the docks, and immediately opposite my troop of tanks was a public house. It was a warm evening and some of the locals were gathered outside supping their drinks. This was an opportunity too good to miss, so with the permission of our troop leader we nipped across a couple at a time to buy bottles of beer and bags of crisps from the bottle and jug bar. It was as if we were going on a picnic. Some picnic!

While I was munching crisps, and washing them down with intermittent swigs from the first of six half-pint bottles of pale ale, a thought struck me. I would save two of the bottles and vowed to myself that if, please God, Tom and I survived to see the end of the war, we could drink these, wherever we were at the time, in a victory toast. I there and then put them in with some other possessions I kept in a small empty metal ammunition box in the turret.

That deed done, I prised the crown cork cap off the next bottle of ale with the tin-opener blade in my jack-knife, and downed it whilst tuning the dial of the A-set to get some music. I lingered awhile on the frequency of a foreign station, listening to the lilting strains of 'Lili Marlene' being sung by a woman in a language unknown to me. Not surprising really, as I never progressed beyond native English! As the song faded out, I twiddled the knob to get the BBC nine o'clock news; but just as Big Ben was chiming the hour my tank commander returned from a meeting with the troop officer and, with a circling motion of his right arm above his head, intimated that it was time to roll on. I never did hear the latest news, as I immediately tuned the B-set back to the required frequency.

The civvies outside the pub waved at us and shouted words of encouragement, but their cries were soon drowned by the noise of tank engines as our troop moved off towards the entrance to the dock.

This was the start of the greatest adventure of my life, and my feeling of apprehension at what lay ahead was heavily outweighed by a far greater sense of excitement now welling up inside me. I was going to take part in battles that would make the news on the radio and in the papers, rather than just read or listen to the reports as I'd done in the past. I was going to see some action at last!

Chapter 5

The Normandy Beaches

I peered around me in the below-decks gloom of the LCT. The place was beginning to look like a sick bay, literally, and starting to smell a bit, so I suggested to Joe that we go up on deck for some fresh air. The wind was very keen and we held on to the rails. We could just about see the sea around us, and felt the spray thrown up over the side of the ship as it churned its way through the choppy waters of the English Channel.

We made our way to the stern and joined some of our lads already there. One of the ship's crew was dishing out large enamel mugs of hot cocoa, fresh from the galley. Another seaman arrived with a welcome snack of cheese and corned beef sandwiches. I took a sandwich of bully beef in thick chunks of bread, not knowing it would be the last piece of bread to enter my mouth for many weeks - hard tack biscuits from our composite ration boxes were yet to come. Joe and I gratefully thanked the seaman refilling our mugs with more hot cocoa. We were joined by our two troop officers, coming along for refreshments after a conversation with the ship's captain up on the bridge.

The sailor told us it was much quieter on the beaches nowadays. 'More like Southsea on a cold March day in comparison with the D-Day landings.' Who's he kidding, I thought to myself. He's just trying to cheer us up.

'Still, I'd rather be on a ship than in one of your sardine tins,' he went on, pursing his lips. 'I hear they can brew up quicker than our cook can!' This bit of instantaneous wit brought laughter from the tank men.

'Well, I don't think some of our lads down below throwing up in their sick bags would agree with you. They'd certainly prefer being in a tank than a ship,' I remarked. My troop leader turned to question me, and I could see the concern on his face. Both officers then decided to visit the men and see what they could do to comfort them, while we looked around us in the gradually increasing dawn light.

In the darkness of night I had thought our LCT was alone, but now in the half-light we began to see little dots appear in the sea around us. As it got lighter the dots took on the shape of ships – everywhere, all around us, as far as the eye could see! It was an incredible sight to behold, and most uplifting to our morale. We weren't isolated, as we had felt, but part of a huge armada conveying the various units with their tanks, transport, equipment and stores to reinforce the beachhead. I wondered if there would still be room enough left there to put us all!

Gradually we could discern the coastline of Normandy taking shape as we steamed onwards at a fair rate of knots. Then, slowly coming into view and getting larger every minute, a huge warship, which had all the tank crews lining up on the port side of the LCT to gaze and wonder. It was the battleship HMS *Rodney*, anchored broadside on to the coast with her huge guns pointing towards land, ready for action. The lads cheered and waved in unison as we passed by, breaking the uncanny silence.

As we got nearer to land we could see silver reflections from the early morning sun shining on barrage balloons in the sky. Then we could see the spire of a church, houses, buildings. We passed a line of very big ships anchored offshore, with their cargoes being unloaded on to smaller craft for transmission to the beaches. It all looked so impressive and well organised.

We watched this scenario with some incredulity. It was difficult to imagine that we were actually approaching the beaches of Normandy. Where was Goering's vaunted Luftwaffe, with their dreaded dive-bombers? The shells from enemy artillery? The mayhem of naked war we had all been expecting on our arrival? The absence of enemy activity in the area was most gratifying, and acted like a tonic on those who had been unwell. Perhaps a little bit of fear affected some of them, apart from the sea sickness, but they now had the colour back in their cheeks again and were laughing and joking with the rest of us.

Just then we were startled by the sound of heavy gunfire, seemingly just behind us, which confirmed that we were really in the battle zone. 'That's *Rodney*'s guns,' said a nearby seaman, amused at our instinctive reaction to the sudden gunfire. 'Don't worry, they won't fall short,' he added with a chuckle.

My officer assumed an air of nonchalance, as if being directly under the fire of a battleship's big guns was an everyday occurrence. His sangfroid air may have convinced the sailor, but he didn't fool our lads as, with a smug look on his face, he disappeared up onto the bridge.

Soon the ship began to reduce speed, and tank crews were ordered down below by troop sergeants to prepare for disembarking. While we were busy at our various tasks the LCT increased its speed, but shortly afterwards we were all thrown forward as the ship shuddered and stopped. According to a sailor down below with us we had hit a sandbank. Then, with the engines roaring away and sending vibrations through even our tanks, the ship backed out. It went into reverse for quite a while, amidst gleeful shouts from the lads about going home again; then further mocking as the ship went forward once more at quite some speed. It spurted towards the beach, landed right up to the shore, and stayed put.

'Straight ahead for Bernières-sur-Mer for you, and back to Pompey for us,' said the sailor, as we waited for the bow ramp door to be lowered. But when the ramp came down it dropped right onto the beach itself – the biggest anti-climax one could ever have imagined, landing dry-shod on Juno beach, with nothing to disturb the morning calm other than the clatter and shouts of beach working parties. All those weeks spent hard at work at Headley waterproofing our tanks.... Visions of driving our tanks through deep water and up onto the beach amidst enemy fire with our guns blazing.... Yet here we were on the beach, and not even the tracks on our tanks getting wet. We felt cheated!

As my tank drove down the ramp and came to a halt a little

way from the water's edge, I impulsively grabbed my first souvenir of France. Emptying the few sticks left in a box of Ship matches (a very appropriate brand in the circumstances), I jumped down from the tank onto the beach and filled the box with sand. It was part of the soil upon which Hitler swore the British would never set foot, and I had to have some! While I was down on my haunches filling the matchbox the rest of the crew dismounted, and subjected me to a barrage of jokes about seaside holidays. I tried to explain that I wanted the sand as a souvenir, but they couldn't see the point. To them the sand was the same as on any British beach. For me, however, it was a symbol to be treasured. Normandy sand. French soil.

I clambered back into the turret to put my precious matchbox in my metal ammunition box, and was just rejoining the crew when a sudden explosion had us diving for cover at the rear of the tank. I instantly thought it was an enemy shell, or perhaps a mine had been triggered off; whatever it was, it was too close for comfort. On hearing a commotion just ahead of us, we ventured a peep out from behind our tank. There were traces of smoke rising up from the tank in front, and bits and pieces of waterproofing material littered the beach around it. Digweed, the gunner, jumped down from the tank, his hand streaming blood. He looked up at the tank, stunned, and said, 'Well, it worked, didn't it! What silly bleeder done that?'

We guessed what had happened. We had removed the sealing around the drivers' visors, as ordered, but the rest was to be removed when we reached the tank harbour inland. Someone had inadvertently pressed the switch in the driver's compartment, detonating the cordtex and thereby blowing off all the waterproof sealing and nearly Digweed's hand. He achieved immortality by being the first casualty in our squadron and, as far as I know, the regiment.

After first aid had been administered to the unfortunate victim, we were ready to move off to join up with our unit somewhere inland. Our two troop officers had meandered off along the beach, endeavouring to locate our regiment's directional sign amongst the myriad on display. They found our exit, an opening about one hundred yards to the right of where we had landed, and returned from their reconnaissance with orders to move.

We drove through a gap in the sea wall, bounded on both sides with white tape to mark the safe passageway through a minefield. Signboards reading *ACHTUNG - MINEN!* carried the shape of a skull and crossbones for the benefit of those not understanding the language. Safely through the mined area, I gazed around in great curiosity from my perch in the turret, taking in everything as we rumbled on up a lane. This was my first glimpse of a foreign country, but we might just as well have been back in the Kent countryside: green meadows bounded by hedges and ditches; trees and copses; farm houses here and there; apple trees. Only the grazing cows seemed a little different: a piebald reddish-brown and white, and unlike the mixed coloured herds I'd seen in England.

As we passed near one farmyard I saw my first French person, a young woman. Her response to our shouts of greeting was a frosty stare, thus confirming reports we'd heard that not all the natives in this area were falling over themselves to welcome the 'liberators'. We were, in fact, to find a mixed reception wherever we went in Normandy, although some could be forgiven for their animosity. Whole villages had been wrecked, with dwellings reduced to rubble from the bombardments and ground fighting between the combatants, and livestock killed or lost. This could not be quickly forgotten by the unfortunate people caught up in the line of battle. There were those, also, whose lucrative practices in collaborating with the Germans were brought to an end by the Allied invasion. They not only resented us, but also went in fear of being betrayed and dealt with by the Maquis.

As we journeyed along through the rear areas of the beachhead, past the supply depots and artillery positions, we saw ample evidence of earlier battles, and the temporary graves of those who had fallen in action. Mounds of earth, each with a rough wooden cross and rifle stuck in the ground, and the dead man's helmet on top. We looked at these graves with morbid curiosity; they contrasted oddly with the grubby-looking soldiers going about their tasks in apparent oblivion.

I describe these men as 'grubby' to illustrate the fact that we, who had only landed a few hours ago, looked like new pins in comparison. Indeed, one soldier shouted up to us, 'You lot look as if you've just left the parade ground at Catterick. You'll soon lose some of that polish here.' Cheeky monkey! His saucy remarks were accurate enough, though, as we did look very smart. We'd managed to get a wash and brush-up on the LCT that morning, and the King's Own regimental cap badges shone like burnished gold on our black berets. Even our tanks looked as if they'd just come off the assembly lines at Vauxhall Motors, and the names painted in large yellow letters on their sides could be seen a mile away.

We soon encountered some large signs, with the warning DUST BRINGS SHELLS, as we went past a field in which we could perceive some big Royal Artillery guns under camouflage. The tanks did ease up but couldn't keep the dust clouds down, much to the chagrin of the RA lads, who were frantically pointing to the signs and shouting obscenities at us. As newcomers, we were at that stage too polite to give them a two-fingered salute in response!

Eventually the leading troop officer found our unit sign, a white 53 on a green square, at the entrance to a large field. We were here at last: the 107 Regiment harbour. The lads already there must have heard our tank engines roaring away long before we got there, and each tank got a cheer as we entered, plus some ribald comments about our late arrival. I had eyes for only one among the reception committee: my twin brother. He'd been on my mind ever since we left Waterlooville. Had he made it here safely? I scanned the crowd as my tank drove into the field, and was immediately relieved to spot his happy, smiling face among the throng. There he was, with Bill Powland, Jock Gould and Tommy Reilly, and waving like mad, probably as relieved to see me as I was to see him.

Donk, bless him, was on hand to guide us to our reserved position on the perimeter of the field, and Tom rushed over to greet me. As I got out of the turret and jumped down beside him, he grabbed hold of me and gave me a bear hug. It was a wonderful reunion, although we had only been apart since early the previous day - in between had been the journey into the unknown, across the hazardous waters of the Channel and landing on the Normandy beaches.

We compared notes on our crossings. Tom, it transpired, had travelled on a big American LST and landed on the beach at Courseulles, after enjoying plenty of good food and all mod cons aboard. Bully for you lot, I thought.

Before we new arrivals could do anything other than park our tanks alongside the hedge at suitable intervals, Jock the cook appeared. He must have brewed up as soon as he saw us arrive. With the assistance of Bill Hollowbread, who had driven the cook's truck over, he began filling our mugs with hot, strong tea and handing out pieces of bread pudding. The ever-resourceful Jock had tested his culinary art by making this delicacy using leftovers from the final bread ration received in England. It tasted marvellous!

'That's yer lot,' said Bill with a grin. 'You're on compo rations from now on, like the rest of us.' Rather apologetic and with a rueful look, Jock confirmed Bill's statement in his broad Scots accent. 'Ye feed yersen frae noo on, ye ken.'

We had work to do, removing the waterproof sealing from the tanks. It took only an hour or so to dismantle what had taken us about six weeks to assemble laboriously. There wasn't much else to do after that, though, other than make ourselves as comfortable as possible and wait for a battle in which our services would be required. The field was an ideal spot for summer camping, with a hedge running parallel to the lane on one side and a hedge separating us from an orchard on the other. But somebody, somewhere, sooner or later, would twig that we were here and could be usefully employed elsewhere.

After slinging a camouflage net over the tank and decorating it with leafy branches from adjacent trees until you could hardly differentiate one from the other, my crew erected the bivouac. This consisted of the tank sheet cover lashed over the hull of the tank at the top and pegged to the ground at the bottom, forming a lean-to against the tank's side and giving us protection from the elements. All that remained was to unroll our bedding, already covered in a groundsheet, and stake a claim to a place on the ground. There was just enough space for the five crew members to sleep side by side in reasonable comfort. To make things a bit more like home we rigged up a light using the tank's batteries, and got some music on the radio.

It was time to open our newly-issued box of composite rations and share them out. We gathered round expectantly while Sergeant Ellis prised the lid off the box. He took out the goodies inside and held them up for inspection, to the accompaniment of oohs and ahs from the lads. The box contained everything needed for the sustenance of a troop of 15 men for one day. Individual tinned steak puddings and dessert puddings, which only needed heating up in water. Tins of corned beef, self-heating soup, and evaporated milk. Sugar, soap, toilet paper, matches, cigarettes in round-shaped tins, chocolate, boiled sweets. These items were philosophically accepted, but one thing got a universal thumbs down: the large, flat, round objects, described euphemistically as biscuits, that were to take the place of daily bread in our diet.

I tried one out on the spot at the invitation of the troop officer – or, to put it another way, I was requested to act as a guinea pig to test the hardness and taste, if any, of this thing masquerading as a biscuit. I took a few bites, nearly cracking my front teeth before I was successful in breaking a piece off, then chewed away at the hard lump in my mouth, and eventually swallowed it. My saliva was not quite strong enough to dissolve the rock-like substance, however, and it went down my throat in jagged little pieces which only passed by my epiglottis with difficulty.

'Well?' said the officer, as he and the rest of the troop stood there waiting for my reaction.

'Well,' I replied, after recovering from the shock and the realisation that this was to be the substitute for white bread thenceforth. 'They're as hard as iron, and horrible. I reckon they've been left over from the last war – a dog would turn his nose up at them.' The officer poured scorn on my report, but declined my challenge to try one for himself. 'We'll have to find ways to make them more palatable if possible, that's all.'

Taffy suggested we could bombard the enemy with them if we ran short of ammunition; Joe thought they might come in handy as shims (washers); and the troop sergeant proposed that we each keep an iron-hard biscuit in our breast pocket to protect the heart from a bullet. But the biscuits, along with the rest of the compo box, were shared out equally between the troop.

We gorged ourselves, almost finishing the whole day's ration, then retired for the night. The tiring journey and a full belly sent me into a deep sleep no sooner than my head touched my improvised pillow, and the next thing I recall is being shaken by someone amidst cries of 'wakey wakey'. It was morning already, although it seemed as though I'd only had about five minutes' sleep.

Tom came over, accompanied by Punchy Porter, Jock Gould and Tommy Reilly, and invited me to join them on a scrounge to see if we could get some eggs and milk. My crew approved, knowing they would share in the proceeds of the foraging expedition if it proved successful, so we strolled along the narrow lane in search of a farmhouse.

At the first farm we came across we were put off by a huge, fierce-looking Alsatian dog, barking and snarling at us from the other side of an iron gate. It was guarding the entrance to the farmhouse drive, and its need to bite a chunk out of the leg of anyone who opened the gate looked greater than our need of eggs, so we made a hurried exit. 'Ye woodna' hev enna balls left wi' yon beestie,' exclaimed Tommy Reilly.

The next farmhouse looked more promising and was approached by a little bridge over a narrow stream. Everything seemed very quiet as we walked up to the house and knocked on the door, which was surrounded by lovely climbing roses. No answer, so we tried again, this time a bit louder. Still no luck. Then, seeing what looked suspiciously like a WC cistern chain with a ball at its end hanging on the doorframe, I tried a pull to see if it 'flushed' someone out. A bell rang on the inside loud enough to wake the dead, and the door was opened almost immediately by a medium height, stocky man, wearing a black beret and with a thick moustache covering his entire upper lip right up to just under the nose. He bore a marked resemblance to Lieutenant Colonel Rowe, the previous OC of 107 Regiment.

As not one of us knew a word of French it was going to be difficult to communicate. Tom started off by asking if he understood English - there was always a million to one chance that he could. But the man made no response, nor to our enquiry in English as to whether he had any eggs. So I got down on my haunches, made the sort of straining noise I imagined a chicken would make when laying an egg, put my hand under my bottom and held up an imaginary egg between my thumb and forefinger. The man paused for a moment in contemplation of the meaning of this charade, then a glimmer of recognition crossed his face. He came out of the house and beckoned us to follow him to the farmyard at the rear of the house, where he opened a door to reveal a dirty old WC. Pointing to a bucket of water standing under a dripping water tap by the wall, he went through the motions of emptying the bucket down the WC to flush it.

Punchy doubled up in fits at the idea that I'd mimed using a toilet. The man appeared puzzled at our laughter, but seemed to realise he had misconstrued my acting performance. He just shrugged his shoulders and muttered some words in French, which I imagined were a suggestion that we have another go.

Tom tried next, pointing to some chickens scratching about in the ground on the other side of the yard and adopting the same posture as I'd done while shouting 'Cock-a-doodle-doo!'. Punchy burst into laughter again at the thought of cockerels laying eggs, but Tom hadn't finished his act. He went through the motions of breaking the top of an imaginary egg, peeling it, and eating the contents with a spoon.

The man concentrated his mind on the meaning of this performance, then suddenly shot his arms up into the air and shouted something in French. It sounded like *WEE - ORFS*, and Punchy thought he was telling us to 'piss orf'. But the man motioned us to follow him to a barn, where he went inside and came out immediately with a satisfied expression on his face, triumphantly holding up an egg. He pointed at the egg and said the French word *'oeuf'*, which sounded to us like *ERF*. We all nodded, and got down to the question of barter. We'd come with plenty of cigarettes, chocolate and soap for exchange, so we each held up so much as a starter. The man responded by walking along a long row of nesting boxes, putting any eggs he gathered into a basket.

Having procured enough eggs, getting fresh milk proved much easier. Tom just gave a few moos, went through the motion of milking a cow with up and down movements of his hands, and picked up the container we'd brought along to hold aloft in front of the man. The farmer beamed in recognition, and we followed him to a cow shed. More cigarettes were produced and the man filled up all our containers with milk from a churn, bringing our initial attempt at the art of barter in a foreign country to a successful conclusion.

The transactions became progressively easier as the days went by and we acquired a smattering of the language. Like many thousands of my compatriots in the forces, I soon found a ready market for our goods in each country we travelled through. Shortages had brought a thriving black market everywhere in Europe for those willing to take the risk - and officers participated as well as the other ranks. I didn't have to draw a penny of army pay for the whole time I was on the continent, so it built up into a nice little nest-egg at the end of my service. I looked on it as a perk.

I was welcomed with open arms by my crew when they saw what I'd brought back for them, and the freshly-laid eggs were boiled without further ado. They tasted delicious, but were not complemented by our biscuits. You can't make 'soldiers' to dip in your egg from hard tack biscuits!

We had visitors that morning, whose shoulder flashes of a black bull on a yellow ground indicated they were from units of the 11th Armoured Division. They had apparently only recently been pulled out of the line, and were resting in the area. We were mocked at first for our late arrival on the scene, but after the jokes came the serious discussions.

They told us not to underestimate the Germans, who were very good fighters - especially the fanatical SS, who would fight to the last man. We also learned, to our dismay, of the devastating effects of the German 88mm high velocity guns, mounted SPs, anti-tank guns, and Tiger tanks. The shells apparently went through our Shermans like a knife through butter. Hearing that our tank guns were 75mm, they disconcerted us still further by commenting that these would be about as much good against the Jerry tanks as a pea shooter.

'You'll have to get real close to 'em to do any harm. You'll never penetrate the Panthers and Tigers with that unless you get real close to 'em. Their frontal armour is almost impregnable!'

The more they elaborated, the more we began to realise that we were outgunned, and less well protected by tank armour than our adversaries. We were advised to use cover to get near them, and shoot them broadside on. The enemy 88mm shells, on the other hand, could apparently penetrate a Churchill about a mile away. The one weak spot in the front of a Panther, we were informed, was a small spot above the driver's head. If you could get a hit there, you might penetrate the front from a couple of hundred yards away. As much chance of doing that, I thought, as threading a needle blindfold.

After these 'veterans' of a few weeks' fighting had left, our lads put some pointed questions to the troop officer regarding our vulnerability against the enemy tanks. He tried to allay our fears to the best of his ability. We had the edge when it came to manoeuvrability: the Tiger was a monster of a tank, about 15 tons heavier than our Churchills, and rather cumbersome to manoeuvre quickly. The Panther was a fast tank, but had a slow traversing turret. We should have to outwit them and be 'foxy', that was all. He did his best to revive our flagging morale, telling us not to sell ourselves short as we had a good tank which had proved itself in earlier fighting in close combat, but the doubts remained.

We learned later that our officers paid a call on their opposite numbers in the 11th Armoured Division to pick their brains on battle tactics against the enemy armour and get all the information they could to help us when we would, inevitably, confront the enemy in battle. In the meantime we whiled away the days as best we could in our own little Normandy field. The peace was only broken occasionally by heavy barrages from big guns in our nearby artillery batteries, or Allied aircraft roaming the skies above on their various missions.

The troop officers lived and slept with their crews, which proved a great leveller. No matter what their former background or lifestyle, the officers mucked in wholeheartedly with the other ranks, and this tended to increase our respect for them if anything. We welcomed the new relationship, and didn't take any liberties with the officers; it was always 'sir' and never a Christian name, so discipline was in no way impaired.

On one of our foraging expeditions we managed to procure some Calvados, the strong local tipple, and cider from the largest barrel I had ever seen. The owner put a chalk mark on the front of the barrel for each large jug of cider he poured out of the tap – and he made quite a few chalk marks during our stay in the area! Our evenings were therefore quite jolly, with Tommy Reilly and myself playing for sing-songs.

I was fortunate to be able to visit Bayeux one day, when a three tonner had to be taken to a transport depot near the town and replaced. We passed villages on the way that had been reduced to rubble, and one felt sad at the price paid by the inhabitants for liberation from the Germans. I was also struck by the number of holy statues dotting the roadside: at almost every crossroads I saw a statue of the Blessed Virgin Mary with a baby Jesus, or Jesus Christ crucified on the cross, and, amazingly, always tended with fresh flowers. It also seemed strange to me to be speeding along the main road on the right-hand side instead of the left.

After changing over the three tonner we went into Bayeux for a look around the town. It was crowded with Allied troops, but we saw no sign of war damage as the town had been evacuated by the Germans immediately after the invasion. We walked through the cobbled streets, bedecked with national flags, and made our way towards the cathedral, where we mingled with sightseers whilst the enterprising local English-speaking 'guides' recounted the cathedral's history in return for cigarettes. The Bayeux Tapestry was not on display, though, as it had been hidden away in a place of safety and not yet reinstated.

We received the call to arms on Thursday 6 July, and there was

3. On leave after VE Day: Eileen, Phyllis, Tom and Steve.

4. Churchill tanks in N.W. Europe, 1945.

great excitement at our squadron harbour. Montgomery was mounting an operation to capture Caen. The squadron was all keyed-up and ready to do battle as we left the harbour for the front line, and travelled to another field situated near the River Mue, where we were to hold ourselves in readiness.

That day I saw the first of what my Dad would have called 'good Germans': dead ones! Crossing over railway lines which had been the scene of recent action, we found German corpses lying around in grotesque positions, presumably just where they had fallen in battle. Their skins had turned a blue-black colour and their faces were contorted, as though in agony at death. It was a hot day and swarms of flies were buzzing around the bodies. There were obvious signs that human vultures had been at work: pockets were turned inside out, and a couple of corpses didn't even have boots – probably taken by 'Froggies' in the wake of the battle.

I looked at them with morbid curiosity. It was all rather eerie. The only dead person I'd seen before was one of my uncles. He had lain in peace, in a coffin placed on trestles in the parlour, with a serene expression on his face. It was a stark contrast to the dead bodies here on the battlefield.

We erected our bivouacs, although we slept restlessly in our excitement, and then watched hundreds of Halifax and Lancaster bombers flying over to drop their bombs on Caen at sunset the following day. That night there was a massive and deafening artillery bombardment on the northern defences of the unfortunate town; but although our regiment was on standby for the battle, we weren't called on to fight. It was disappointing, really, after getting all worked up; like taking your harp to a party and not being asked to play. By 9 July everything was over, and half of Caen had been captured by British forces.

During the fighting we were moved around a bit, and did at least get the feel of the battle zone. At one point we saw a line of prisoners being shepherded along by our infantry: the older men shuffling along slowly, looking rather forlorn, wearing greatcoats down to their ankles; the younger element truculent, and making rude signs at us as they passed by our stationary tanks. So this was the enemy. They didn't look a bit like the jackboot-clad, goose-stepping troops I'd seen countless times on cinema newsreels.

As the line of prisoners halted temporarily, on an impulse I jumped down from the tank and motioned to one of them to undo his belt with its eagle buckle. I wanted it as a souvenir for my nephew. As the man took off the belt and handed it to me his trousers started to fall down, and he held them up as he marched off. I felt rather ashamed of myself at that moment.

On 10 July we witnessed our first live action. We were on a hilltop overlooking Carpiquet airfield, and had a grandstand view of the Canadians clearing out the last remnants of enemy resistance on its southern edge. After some fierce fighting at close quarters the Canadians were successful, and the airfield was in Allied hands.

Although we didn't fire a shot the whole time we were on standby, we went into Caen before returning to our original harbour. It was a real shambles. The unfortunate inhabitants had been living in their cellars during the bombardment and subsequent fighting, and weren't too overjoyed to see us - their thankfulness at their liberation from the Germans was mixed with anger at their lovely town being razed to the ground. I walked amidst the ruins of Le Bon Sauveur convent with a feeling of shame: the bombing of this holy place seemed sacrilegious.

Our trip to the front line had been enlightening, in that we experienced the unique sounds and smells that go hand in hand with battle, and the death and destruction it entails. The stench of decomposing cattle, mixed with the smell of explosives, hung in the air. Fast staccato bursts from the enemy's Spandau machine guns were easily distinguishable from the far slower fire of British Bren guns. The sounds of exploding shells and mortar bombs were too near for comfort, especially when you were only on standby!

We'd also seen the British beachhead defences in depth on our travels to and from the front. Infantry was dug in at intervals, with well-concealed anti-tank guns at vital spots. Medium and heavy artillery batteries were equally well camouflaged. And what with field artillery, the big guns of offshore ships joining in the bombardment, plus almost unopposed bombing by the Allied airforce, it was clear that the enemy would never be able to break the line. In the few weeks from D-Day the Allies had landed about half a million men and a vast amount of equipment and stores. We were in an unassailable position, and it was now only a question of time before we broke through their line on the American western flank as Monty planned.

The US First Army had launched an attack on 3 July to start the breakthrough, but had found it hard going through the difficult *bocage* area, with its small, high-banked fields and close hedgerows topped with trees. The advance came to a standstill a week later, after the enemy pushed in substantial reserves of armour.

To break the stalemate, Monty planned another operation, codenamed Goodwood, to draw the bulk of the enemy armour away from the Americans and into the Caen area. Eighth Corps, with three armoured divisions under command, was to strike through the Orne bridgehead on 18 July, south towards Falaise. Prior to this, Operation Greenline would start on 15 July with a series of feint attacks by 12th and 30th Corps on the right of 8th Corps, to draw off the enemy armour. My unit, the 34th Tank Brigade, was to have its initiation in this operation after missing the fighting at Caen. To facilitate this, the 31st Tank Brigade (less one regiment) and 34th Tank Brigade were released by 1st Corps and came back under command of 12th Corps on 13 July.

Before I recount the first of my personal experiences in action with 107 Regiment, I would say that an individual's part in a battle seems infinitesimally insignificant. But it is the amount of sacrifice, tenacity and courage the individual can display under great pressure, welded together hundreds of times in a unit, that determines defeat or victory on the battlefield. The private or the trooper doesn't know much about the part he is playing, with his platoon, company, troop or squadron, in the wider context of the battle. He just does what he is ordered, and that's it. In our troop, for instance, I recall the tank commanders returning from briefings and synchronising watches. They would then briefly tell the crew that we were to attack a certain target; we would mount up; and, in liaison with the infantry, fight our way forward to the objective. It is gratifying, therefore, that the individual can in some cases learn from historians' books about the part his unit played in various actions, and how it related to the outcome of the battle.

So, the 34th Tank Brigade were to be committed for the first time, to begin a series of raids on enemy positions and tie down as much enemy armour as possible on 12th Corps' front. My regiment, 107 RAC, was the first to go into action. Our objective was to capture the hamlet of Bon Repos and the village of Esquay. A and B Squadrons, with two troops of Churchill Crocodile flame-throwing tanks from 141 RAC, were to support the attacking infantry of the 2nd Glasgow Highlanders. We were to advance down the forward slopes of Hill 112 with C Squadron in reserve, and assist the infantry as necessary in the battle.

Chapter 6

The Battles for Hill 112

The regiment left harbour on 14 July to travel to the assembly area, with a mixture of excitement and trepidation at the prospect of what would, for the vast majority, be our first taste of action. We could have been given a less daunting initiation than the notorious Hill 112! We'd heard bloodcurdling tales from those who'd been in action there, in the fiercest fighting so far, in the campaign for possession of the vital high ground. Tiger tanks, SP guns and dug-in anti-tank guns had taken a heavy toll of British armour, with their 88mm high velocity AP shells ripping through our tanks like red hot pokers through a slab of butter. We developed an 88mm complex even before we started.

We moved off along the route leading to the salient on the other side of the River Odon, at the tip of which were the northern slopes of Hill 112. The bridgehead had been established by units of the 23rd Hussars and 8th Rifle Brigade on 28 June. Each squadron maintained a reasonable distance from the next as we rolled along the roads across the crowded beachhead, with ammunition and fuel dumps on all sides. Bulldozers had been used to clear a path through the ruins of several villages, with the inevitable MP directing the traffic amidst clouds of dust. We halted for a short break at the ruined village of Cheux.

As I surveyed the rubble of what was once a cottage, I noticed a coloured object on the side window ledge of a shattered room. I climbed over the rubble for a closer inspection, and saw it was a statue of the Blessed Virgin Mary, about nine inches high. It had survived the battering and was coated with dust. As a Roman

Catholic I found this symbolic, and I just had to take it to save it from being damaged in any subsequent action. After cleaning with a damp rag the statue looked shiny and new again, and I made a vow then to keep it with me in the tank until the end, whichever way things went. I jammed the statue up between the smoke bomb ejector and the turret wall, where I could see it and offer it prayers for safety in battle. The regiment assembled that night at Mouen.

Just before the squadron crossed the River Odon the next day we came under shell fire, but fortunately we could see the shells were falling short of target by the eruptions in the earth not far away. It was a fine, dry day, and the tell-tale clouds of dust made by a tank regiment on the move had been an invitation to the enemy artillery to welcome us to the bridgehead. The dug-in Allied infantry took a dim view of our presence and blamed us for the enemy bombardment, if their gesticulations at us were anything to go by. You couldn't blame them - the missiles were landing nearer to them than us.

After crossing the river safely we drove past the ruins of the village of Baron, now reduced to vast heaps of rubble by shelling from both sides. Everywhere around us the fields were pockmarked with shell holes like a lunar landscape. Trees were naked, their branches battered by the constant shelling. This most inhospitable spot was our assembly area, and we were brought to a halt in what looked like a graveyard for tanks, SP guns and motorised transport, both ours and theirs. It was also a graveyard for many men who had fallen in battles for the vital high plateau of Hill 112, and I wondered who among those just arriving would be joining them.

My morbid speculation lasted only a fleeting moment, though, as there was work to be done. We unloaded four-gallon jerrycans from a fuel truck which arrived soon after us, and topped up our tanks with petrol immediately: we'd run low after the journey, but we were now in the front line and had to be prepared to move backwards or forwards at the drop of a hat. The next priority was feeding the inner man from the by-now hated selection of 'same again' tinned food and hard biscuits in the composite ration box. My grandmother used to admonish us kids, when we turned up our noses at the plates of tripe and cow heel she put in front of us, by saying we would eat anything if we were hungry. How right she was: our hunger would always overcome our dislike of the repetitive fare in the compo box. But how I would have relished Gran Murphy's delicacy, served up steaming hot on a plate!

After the meal, I joined some of the others inspecting a knocked-out Tiger tank about thirty yards from where our troop had parked. A formidable monster, it looked much larger than our Churchills and half as heavy again. It was a real Tiger, the real McCoy, in comparison with the almost-as-large Panther tank, with a long gun, which we had previously sometimes mistaken for a Tiger. But there was no doubt now, as we gazed up at its huge long gun which wouldn't have looked out of place on the *Rodney*, that here was the object of our nightmares. Estimating its frontal armour to be six or seven inches thick, we couldn't imagine how anything we had on our side could penetrate it - except perhaps a medium artillery field gun at about ten yards! But a neat hole made by an AP shell penetrating this tank's thick armour had caused the brew up. The British tank crew, or anti-tank gun crew, must have seen the whites of their eyes before firing, but it was proof that the dreaded Tiger could be knocked out and thus a little fillip to us. We could be confronted by one any time now, from the SS Panzer units in possession of the areas at the bottom of the southern slopes of Hill 112.

We stayed inside our tanks that day, trying to get a bit of sleep, and not daring to move out in case another sudden 'stonk' of shells rained down on us. On that evening, Saturday 15 July, the tanks of A and B Squadrons drove up the northern slope of Hill 112 to the attack start lines.

We halted just below the crest of the hill where the infantry of the 2nd Glasgow Highlanders, whom we were to support in the attack, were dug in among a shell-battered copse. It soon became evident from the reaction of the Highlanders that we were making too much noise and dust as we got into position: one of their NCOs came storming over to my troop and tore us off a strip. Sergeant Ellis and I had our heads out of the turret, and removed our headsets as he approached to hear what he was saying, but we could hardly understand a word of the broad Scots accent. We got the gist of it, though: the irate Highlanders were blaming last night's shelling on our arrival. They had a point, too, and with our engine noise and dust clouds rising up into the air like Red Indian smoke signals, we could invite another bout of shelling before the attack got under way.

Our troop officers consulted with the infantry about attack tactics and timing before returning to brief the tank commanders in their respective troops. We then sat in position in our tanks, with hatches closed and an HE shell up the spout, all ready for action. We were extremely pent up, watching the minutes tick by towards the very first second of our very first battle.

It was just getting dark as the Scots lads clambered from their slit trenches and advanced over the crest of the hill down the southern slope, with our tanks following in their wake. Taffy had his eye glued to the telescopic gun sight, ready to fire the 75mm or the Besa machine gun in a split second at any specified target. I was standing by, ready to reload shells into the gun as fast as Taffy could fire them. Sergeant Ellis gave Joe directions for the advance over the intercom. We were all as tense and scared as foxes scenting hounds, expecting to be met with a hail of 88s the instant our tanks went over the top of the hill.

But all was quiet: our artillery had thoughtfully put down a huge smoke-screen to hide us from the enemy gunners, and they couldn't see us. Looking through my periscope in the turret, the smoke made it difficult to see very much. I could just about discern a little road to our right leading down to our first objective, the hamlet of Bon Repos. Perhaps the smoke had been a little overdone by the artillery - it was good cover for us but, on the other hand, we couldn't see either. Taffy had an itchy trigger finger, but not a target could be seen.

A little way down the hill, just off the road, we saw some flamethrowers from the two troops of 141 Regiment's Churchill Crocodile tanks going into action. They were squirting fiery liquid at the ruins of a house, and the flames lit up the scene. I could see ghost-like figures of infantry moving about and probing their way forwards, lit intermittently by the flames.

Sergeant Ellis was swivelling his periscope around, trying to spot any likely targets. We heard a report from another tank over the A-set: they had just seen the tank in front of them brew up. I looked over to Sergeant Ellis and saw the concern on his face at this bad news. I had a gripping feeling in my stomach and my mouth went dry: the subconscious inner fear of death which I imagine is felt by everyone taking part in their first battle. I was in terror, at that moment, of our tank being brewed up by a dreaded 88mm AP shell from a tank or anti-tank gun, and being burnt to a cinder. I was to find this fear getting a little less with each subsequent battle. It's all a question of an individual's will-power and fatalistic acceptance of the situation.

Above the messages over the radio headsets, with orders flowing to and fro between the various commanders, I could hear the sounds of battle. There was lots of small arms fire, especially the distinctive bursts from Spandau machine guns, and cracks from tank and anti-tank guns. I could see tracer bullets whizzing in all directions as I looked through my periscope. Then something hit the turret with a loud ping, and the sound reverberated in the confined space. Sergeant Ellis rapidly twiddled his periscope, then suddenly shouted across to me that he had seen the flash of an 88, and ordered the gunner to traverse left. As Taffy did so, Ellis shouted to him to stop. I looked through my periscope in the direction in which our gun was pointing, saw a flash, and in a split second Ellis shouted, 'Fire!'

The gun should have recoiled back into the turret after firing the HE shell from the breech block, but it didn't. It was a misfire! Taffy was pulling at the trigger and cursing in rapid Welsh while I yanked at the lever to open the breech block, but it was stuck. Taffy picked up the hammer kept for this type of emergency and tapped the underside of the block, giving me a rap on the knuckles in his haste, but I was too busy at the time to notice the pain. After a couple of knocks I opened the breech block and removed the shell, which I gingerly disposed of through the hatch, my heart in my mouth all the time. I immediately reloaded with another

HE and Taffy promptly fired the gun, successfully this time. All this took only a few seconds, and I could see the flame from the explosion as our 75mm HE shell hit, hopefully on target. I offered a prayer to the statue of the Blessed Virgin Mary that we had put a suspected anti-tank gun out of action.

Down at the foot of the hill we halted a short way before the little collection of buildings which formed our objective. The smoke was lifting here and there, and we could see A Squadron's tanks to our right. We put in a few bursts of Besa fire at the request of the infantry, raking the specified targets from side to side, after which it was the turn of the flamethrowers once again. Then the Glasgow Highlanders advanced, and disappeared into the smoke and flames of the burning buildings in search of the enemy.

We waited in our tanks, feeling as insecure as an art model on her first nude assignment, with shells bursting around us all the while. After what seemed like an eternity we caught sight of the enemy: Taffy had his trigger finger ready on the Besa, but it wasn't necessary. They were coming along the road with their hands held high, shepherded by some Jocks with rifles and fixed bayonets.

Bon Repos had been captured and held by the Highlanders, but it wasn't until Esquay was taken too that A and B Squadrons were released by the infantry. We didn't hang about!

Our artillery friends lobbed over another smoke-screen to cover our withdrawal, which was once again a bit overdone, so it was like blind man's bluff heading back up the hill, groping our way through the smoke with the turret gun over our tails. We were lost, and we weren't the only ones, judging by the frantic messages coming over the radio. We were told to follow the searchlight, but we could see two, in diametrically opposite directions - one presumably put up by the wily enemy to confuse us after intercepting our radio instruction from RHQ. We thought we were all right as long as we kept moving uphill, although it was like going through the smog of a London pea-souper. Coming out of the smoke we found ourselves too far over to the left and entering a copse - and then it happened!

A terrific explosion sent a shudder through the tank, and it stopped dead. So, for a split second, did my heart, fearing we'd been hit by an 88mm. I've never reacted to anything as fast as I did on that occasion, shooting out of the hatch above me almost as quickly as a 75mm shell leaving our gun barrel. Sergeant Ellis scrambled out of the hatch on his side, followed by Taffy and the rest of the crew. We were drilled to wait for the tank commander's order before abandoning the tank, but in action that's a joke. Ask anybody whose tank had been hit by a shell, or gone up on a mine. The survival instinct ignores the rules and asserts itself instantly at the moment of impact. Countless numbers of tank crews owe their lives to the speed in which they reacted, instinctively, to danger. For the record, anyway, my tank commander didn't utter a word before the frantic exit from the turret - which goes to prove my point!

The crew ran after Sergeant Ellis like 100 metre sprint finalists in the Olympics, hoping he knew where he was going. We raced up the last part of the hill, spurred on even faster by the burping sounds of a Spandau in the distance, and eventually stopped at a copse on the other side of the hill. We were relieved to find ourselves back among the dug-in positions of the Glasgow Highlanders, but the five of us were still in a state of shock. We sat down side by side, on the trunk of a fallen tree, to recover our breath and give vent to our feelings in between gasps for air.

Owen had no doubt that we'd been hit by an 88. Recovering my senses a bit, I suggested we'd either been hit by a shell low down or else gone up on a mine. The sergeant and Taffy both agreed. I handed round cigarettes from a case I kept in my breast pocket, feeling in urgent need of a drag, but the flickering flame of Joe's cigarette lighter brought a torrent of abuse from the Jocks in their slit trenches. Fearing retribution, we passed round the one ignited cigarette for the others to light theirs. After a few deep draws, inhaling the smoke and nicotine stimulant, we regained our composure. I even began to think about the tank commander's army issue watch, hanging on a hook by the radio and left to the mercy of looters. Why hadn't I 'knocked it off' on the way out? It would have been put down to lost in action anyway - the only officially accepted excuse for losing these oversized, but extremely reliable, pocket watches issued to tank commanders.

I began to rub the knuckles of my left hand, which still felt sore, and warned Taffy to be careful next time he had to hammer the breech block. He retorted with a laugh, saying it was my fault for putting a dud shell in the breech! Sergeant Ellis thought the next shell we fired had put an 88mm anti-tank gun out of action, as there were no flashes afterwards from that direction. We continued to discuss the attack, culminating in the abandonment of *Buzzard*, lying battered on the other side of the hill.

As soon as we arrived back at rear rally we asked which tank had been hit. It was Tommy Turner, whose tank had apparently been knocked out by an 88mm AP from an anti-tank gun. He was the first officer from B Squadron to be killed in action. Two crewmen also died.

Tom was the most relieved among those who welcomed us back, almost jumping for joy when he saw me approaching with the rest of my crew. He'd come along with the driver of the fuel truck to the rear rally point, counted back the tanks, and realised that two had not returned. One was Tommy Turner's, they knew, but the other was unaccounted for until we came back. Sergeant Ellis was given a rocket by our troop officer for abandoning the tank without being able to give a clear indication of the reason for doing so. Was he seriously suggesting that we should have risked life and limb amongst the flying bullets and shells on the other side of the hill to conduct an inquiry? Would *he* have done so?

At first light our crew guided the recovery tank back to where *Buzzard* lay abandoned. In the copse on the other side of the hill we found that the REs had just finished clearing a path through a minefield, into which our tank had obviously strayed, confirming that we had gone up on a mine. The safe area was marked by white tape, so our recovery tank was able to draw up by the side of *Buzzard*. An RE corporal came to tell us there were some anti-personnel mines as well as landmines in the area, so we were very lucky to have escaped injury in our headlong dash through the minefield. We must have had divine guidance.

We surveyed the damage done to the tank by the mine: the track was hanging down from the front sprocket on the driver's side in a right mess, and there were a few marks left by bullets and shrapnel on the tank's surface. While the tank recovery mechanics started repairs, our crew found out what caused the loud ping which had alarmed us during the battle: a groove cut through on the corner of the turret near the smoke bomb ejector. The bare metal was clean and shiny against the grey colour of the tank. It was probably caused by a glancing hit from an 88mm AP shell.

The point of the missile's impact was only a few inches away from the statue of the Virgin Mary I'd placed inside the turret by the smoke bomber. Joe Whelan was also a Roman Catholic and he and I alone knew the significance of this: our prayers to the Blessed Virgin Mary during the battle had been answered. We were astonished.

We inspected the interior of the tank and, to our amazement, everything was in place just as we had left it. Even the watch was still there, ticking away. Those REs must have been saints, because nothing was missing. Our tank recovery mechanics were meanwhile working like beavers on *Buzzard* to make the necessary repairs: we were in no-man's-land, and at the mercy of enemy fire should we be spotted.

As soon as *Buzzard* had been satisfactorily repaired, both tanks raced out of the copse to the top of the hill and over the crest, keeping our fingers crossed all the while – we half-expected a hail of 88mm fire to be launched at us while travelling across the clear ground between the copse and the crest of the hill in full view of enemy observation positions. We made it safely, though, to rejoin the squadron at the rally point.

Having taken part in the capture of Bon Repos and Esquay, it would have been nice to be taken out of the line and rested for a while to recover our nerves. Not a bit of it! The Glasgow Highlanders withdrew from Bon Repos and Esquay that day, much to our astonishment in view of the hard fighting and casualties endured in their recent capture. We supposed there must be a method in the madness somewhere higher up – perhaps a case of keeping the enemy guessing – but meanwhile towards evening we were sent back again to take up position at the top of the reverse slope of Hill 112, as the first line of defence against a counter-attack by the enemy.

Our sister regiment, 153 RAC, embarked on their first assignment on this day; a similar operation to the one in which 107 had taken part the previous day. Supporting the 8th Royal Scots in the attack, the force captured Gavrus and Bougy, but later in the afternoon they were counter-attacked by groups of Tiger and Panther tanks. Listening to reports of the battle on the A-set as we sat in our tank on Hill 112, it all sounded terrifying. We winced each time we heard a Churchill had brewed up. Tank commanders reported sightings of Tigers, Panthers and self-propelled anti-tank guns as the battle continued. The day before we had cursed our luck at being the first regiment in the brigade to take part in the campaign; but as we followed the course of this battle assiduously over the air we considered ourselves fortunate to have been given the honour, in the circumstances.

153 RAC fought hard against the odds, succeeded in wreaking much damage on the enemy counter-attacking forces, and gave no ground. Their casualties were later reported to be 16 officers and 80 other ranks, of whom nine officers, including the CO, Colonel Wood, and 30 other ranks were killed. When the regiment withdrew to refit on the following day, 17 July, only 29 battleworthy tanks had survived.

That was the day the remaining regiment in the brigade, 147 RAC, was committed for the first time, supporting the Jocks in an attack on Evrecy. The enemy were thoroughly on their guard by now, and the town was ferociously defended by SS Panzers with dug-in 88s, Tigers and Panthers. 147 RAC withdrew with a number of prisoners in the bag, but the severe shelling caused many casualties.

The enemy had obviously tracked the movement of our regiment to the assembly area, and bided their time until we were all in position before striking at us that night. Tom was paying me yet another of his many visits from the echelon, about a hundred yards or so away from my troop. One minute we were talking in a little group, and the next the darkness of the night was lit up by myriad floating flares hanging in the sky above us. Like the inexperienced troops we were, we just stood around admiring the spectacle. The sky looked as it had on the night we stood at the Monument in London in the aftermath of a Luftwaffe incendiary attack which left the city in flames.

We soon found out who had laid on the pretty display, as the air was suddenly rent with a rapid series of explosions from shells falling all around us. Everyone instinctively dived for the nearest cover. I dashed underneath a nearby knocked-out Tiger and lay there in a bit of panic, flat on my stomach, my heart racing away, and my arms over the back of my head to protect it from shrapnel. Another couple of lads were beside me, but Tom had evidently rushed off in a different direction.

The shelling went on intermittently for about half an hour, amidst shouts and screams from the injured. When it was apparent that the bombardment had ceased we began to come out of cover, reeling a little at the shock of it all. An ammunition truck was hit and in flames, the ammo exploding and firing off in all directions like a firework display on Guy Fawkes night. A troop sergeant came staggering towards us with a gaping shrapnel wound in his right arm, and we administered first aid as best we could, any squeamishness at the sight of his deep and bloody wound overcome by our desire to help. He and a number of other casualties were then rushed back to the Casualty Clearing Station for treatment.

Three of our comrades failed to reappear after the shelling, including Jock, the squadron cook, that gentle and lovable man, who had been killed instantly where he had taken cover in a shell crater, his head smashed to a pulp. It shook us rigid. He was the first man in B Squadron to be killed on the Normandy campaign, and we hadn't fired a shot.

A temporary grave was dug and Jock was buried on the spot with his body swathed in a blanket. There was a brief service, and we offered up a few prayers as we stood there trying to fight back the tears. Little incidents flashed through my mind, such as Tom and the duck eggs at Headley. I could picture Jock's smiling face and his answer to Tom, 'Boiled, fried or poached, mon?'. It seemed unreal that he was now dead, and his body lay buried in the earth beneath our feet.

This sad ritual was to be carried out many times after that, as our comrades were killed in action. But for sheer emotional shock the very first death in the squadron was the worst experience of them all. I stood next to Tom and thanked God that it was not one of us mourning the other twin.

All the while our tanks sat perched on the top of Hill 112, just below the crest where the Jocks were on constant alert in their slit trenches. We dared not move outside the tank for more than a few minutes, as we were constantly subjected to mortar bomb attacks and shelling without warning. One corporal, caught outside his tank, didn't move quick enough and was injured badly in the leg by flying shrapnel on the first day of our defensive vigil. He was only the first of many such casualties. We sat there in our tanks, like sitting ducks in a shooting gallery, for ten days.

We did everything in the confines of the tank: sleeping, cooking, eating, washing and shaving. Some crews chanced sleeping under their tanks, but our crew decided against it - we'd heard stories of tanks sinking in the ground and crushing those underneath to a slow death. Others reverted to their infantry training, and dug slit trenches by their tanks in which to sleep at night. Being on the small side, I was able to curl up in the tiny space between the gun, the smoke ejector and the radio, like a winkle in its shell. But the sergeant and Taffy were of greater bulk and found things much more difficult: we three in the turret were more cramped than the two in the driver's compartment up front.

I think we must have subconsciously forced ourselves into a state of constipation for a day or two, and when we did venture forth outside for the necessary, it was a very hasty operation. Armed with a spade we would dash to a shell crater, dig a little hole, do our business, and cover it in again. All the while we were tense, and ready to dash back to the tank at the first sign of shelling, finished or not! At one time my trousers nearly fell off in my haste to seek the sanctuary of the tank when disturbed by mortar bombs halfway through performing. We found our empty shell cases ideal for urinating in, and dumped the contents through the hatch, so we didn't have to leave the tank for this function.

As well as feeling the effects of claustrophobia, we found that the stench in the tank was almost unbearable at times during the hot summer days. The foul smell from the carcasses of dead cattle nearby added to the stink of decay emanating from half-buried corpses, disturbed in their last resting places by shelling. Apart from this, unburied human excreta and rotting leftovers of meals were littered all over the place, combining to create a flies' paradise. The masses of writhing maggots produced millions of huge bluebottles which plagued us constantly, not to mention the mosquitoes and other insect pests which thrived in this environment.

But the hardship of living in such squalor was nothing compared to our constant state of mental tension. Apart from frequent 'stonks' of mortar bombs and artillery shelling, there were numerous exchanges of machine gun and small arms fire the moment any movements were seen from either side which might signal a surprise attack. Snipers were ever-present, awaiting any opportunity to test their marksmanship.

After a few days of living under these nerve-wracking conditions, some reached the limit of their endurance. They resorted to subterfuges, like self-inflicted wounds, to get out of the line. These injuries were made to look like accidents: one corporal had a hatch supposedly fall on his fingers, but was seen by his crew to do it on purpose. We saw a troop sergeant, in another troop on our right, being carried away unconscious in a scout car having deliberately inhaled the exhaust fumes of a petrol-driven portable battery charger and suffered carbon monoxide poisoning. We heard later that he recovered, but we never saw him again. Amazingly, he was a tall and tough type, all mouth and trousers back in England during training, so you never can tell. These men were to be pitied, really - they had reached the end of their tether, and couldn't stand any more.

After spending a week under these abominable conditions it was almost a relief to be called upon to mount another attack against Esquay on 23 July, supporting the 4th Battalion, Welsh Regiment, in a sortie to capture some of the SS defenders and bring them in for interrogation. It felt good to be on the move again as we followed the infantry down the hill, under cover of a smoke-screen. I didn't get such bad collywobbles in my stomach this time, although the sense of fear was always present.

Our 75mm gun also behaved impeccably as our tank fired a number of HE shells at a group of houses near a church in the village. Our targets were pointed out to our troop commander liaising with the infantry officers, and at one time our tank had both the Besa machine guns (one in the turret and the other in the co-driver's position) firing simultaneously: the explosive fumes in the tank had us all coughing and made our eyes smart. There was a nasty moment when a Tiger was observed, silhouetted against the flames of a burning building, with its turret traversing the huge barrel of the 88mm gun round towards our tanks. We fired smoke bombs and 75mm APs at it in that order and, whether it suffered damage or not, it wasn't there when the smoke lifted. We didn't stay around to find out either, and sought cover until the infantry needed us again.

We saw a number of prisoners at close quarters, looking very young and the epitome of the SS Panzer fanatical fighters we'd heard about. We were now in combat with them on Hill 112, which they called the Hill of Calvary after a wayside Calvary, the Croix de Filandriers, on a track from Baron in the north. The valley below this was appropriately dubbed Death Valley by our lads.

Having finally been released by the infantry, on the way back to our rallying point we saw some of the more truculent prisoners being given a few taps from the Taffs' rifle butts as they were shepherded along towards captivity. We could also see the debris left lying about in the area: knocked-out tanks and vehicles everywhere; an unburied corpse here and there, probably the result of the present action. The casualty lists on both sides were running into thousands in the battles at Hill 112.

The enemy soon retaliated against our sortie, sending over planes that night to drop a few bombs on our defensive positions, which did nothing to soothe our nerves after our attack against Esquay. The next day they mounted a counter-attack, eventually repulsed by the combined firepower of the infantry and our tanks. One of our Churchills was knocked out during the action, but fortunately the crew managed to evacuate safely.

After ten days at Hill 112, which seemed an eternity to our squadron, with all the activity and duress, we were given a few days' well-earned rest and refit. During this reorganisation Tom was assigned as a regular tank crew member, so he would get his first taste in battle tank by tank with me, if not side by side. The Dyson twins would ride down Hill 112 together.

It was back to our old stamping ground for a repeat performance on 2 August; our third raid against Esquay. We were all beginning to feel like veterans, which is perhaps why this last raid seemed much easier on the nerves than the previous two. One trooper, however, dropped a turret hatch on his hand on the starting line and was sent back - we gave him the benefit of the doubt. We couldn't do the same for a corporal, and a tank commander at that, who suddenly rushed away from his tank and crouched in a ditch, trembling as though shell-shocked. His nerve had snapped completely, and his mind cracked under the pressure: he just couldn't face another attack against the enemy at the bottom of Hill 112.

I could only feel pity as the members of his crew went over and did what they could to comfort him. We all knew the difference between cowardice, as with some of the 'accidental on purpose' injuries, and those unfortunate instances where the psychological pressure became too much to bear - such as this man, and the sergeant who tried to end it all by inhaling carbon monoxide fumes. Both had reached, and gone beyond, the threshold at which their minds were still capable of acting rationally.

Our third attack on Esquay turned out to be the last battle fought on this front by the 34th Tank Brigade. On the same day, 147 Regiment took part in a raid against Bougy, and 153 Regiment was engaged in a raid on Maltot; after which the brigade was withdrawn to prepare for an operation on another front. The brigade's casualties were 37 officers, 210 other ranks and 47 tanks

(16 brewed up) during the operations up to 5 August. But those who fought and survived the battles around Hill 112 could be justly proud that they had played their part in 12 Corps operations to pin down the enemy armour in this sector, as intended, and so assist the planned breakout on the flank of the Allied line.

Chapter 7

The Battle of the River Orne

After our battle at Esquay on 2 August we were all physically and mentally tired out and in need of a rest. The strain of attacking enemy positions, the anguish at the number of our mates killed or injured, the stress of sitting on Hill 112 for ten days under constant shell and mortar fire and with very little sleep, the heat, the stench, the flies, and the cloying mud everywhere when the heavens opened up, had all taken their toll.

But although we expected be taken out of the line for a well-deserved break, this was just wishful thinking. The battle for Normandy was now in its critical last phase, and 34th Tank Brigade could not be spared. It had a vital role to play; but in armoured division style rather than slogging matches at close quarters against SS Panzers. We were to pursue a retreating enemy and mop up any isolated pockets of resistance on the way.

The Americans had broken out of the Cherbourg peninsula, whilst the British had achieved a breakthrough at Caumont. It was a fitting answer to the carping critics who lambasted Monty for being too cautious, especially after the Operation Goodwood battle for Caen had ground to a halt after three days, on 20 July, well short of its objectives.

We fighting troops never lost faith in Monty, nor in his senior officers. They had the responsibility and were using it wisely. It was easier to replace armour and equipment than men, and the heavy casualties were putting a strain on our dwindling reserves. We had no time for armchair critics playing wargames in comfortable surroundings at home and in the USA. Thank God our officers didn't have the cannon-fodder mentality of the brass hats in the Great War. We were up against brave Germans who gave no quarter, we all did our best against the vaunted Panzer armies, and we resented the criticism levelled against Monty and the commander of the British Second Army, Lieutenant General Miles Dempsey.

On Sunday 6 August our regiment assembled at Villers Bocage, captured two days previously by our old friends in the Glasgow Highlanders with support from Churchills of the 6th Guards Tank Brigade. The latter had received their baptism of fire in this recent Operation Bluecoat, the last of the three Churchill tank brigades to be committed. Despite heavy losses, the breakthrough had been achieved and the Germans were in retreat.

Our squadron assembled in a cornfield about half a mile outside the ruins of Villers Bocage. The road leading eastward was snarled up with vehicles like a London traffic jam: tanks, carriers, and scout cars. One wondered how any order could be restored out of the chaos to get us all in the correct positions on the start line for the advance. It was like lining up on the grid prior to the start of a Grand Prix.

I took the opportunity to dash over and have a few words with Tom, who was now in Punchy Porter's troop after his 'blooding' in the last action at Esquay. Tom had come through it all commendably, as I knew he would: his only disappointment was that he was ordered to hold fire on his Besa when some Jerries held up their arms in surrender!

After a lot of shouted instructions from the infantry officers, my troop was given the go ahead. We were all in a lighthearted mood as we set off, with our infantry riding on the back of our tanks and everyone cracking jokes. We felt like the troops with 'Blood and Guts' Patton, the general commanding the American Third Army, who was at that moment leading his forces in a spectacular armoured dash through Brittany.

We moved in a slow procession across the cornfield and through a hedge on to the road to our left. We were advancing hot on the tail of the retreating enemy, so all the tank guns were loaded and ready to fire, and soon individual troops were engaged in actions against enemy stragglers and isolated pockets of resistance. We stopped at intervals to support the infantry on excursions to search farm buildings and any other spots likely to conceal the enemy: they went in with fixed bayonets, prodding about here and there. It reminded me of my days with the East Surreys, searching for enemy parachutists in the fields of Kent, and the scenery here was remarkably similar. But our searches there were often in vain; here we had more luck. The little pockets of enemy unsurprisingly showed a remarkable degree of alacrity in running out with their hands raised and shouting '*Kamerad*' as a troop of tanks with menacing guns and infantry with fixed bayonets approached their hideouts.

We were held up for quite a while at one point, where fast-firing bursts from a Spandau had the infantry diving for cover. Machine gun and rifle fire was coming from some houses on the high ground to our right, on the far side of an orchard, and called for a set piece attack. It was to us like red meat to a lion after the attacks in the half-light against heavily defended positions around Hill 112. Our troop commander liaised with the infantry officer to decide the plan of attack: the troop split up, and each tank went with infantry on a separate route towards the buildings. We fired smoke and sprayed the area with our Besa machine guns; then the infantry quickly dashed forward into the houses and emerged with some prisoners. The enemy toll of casualties was one dead and two injured, one of whom was in a very bad way indeed, but some had managed to get away, taking the Spandau with them.

As battles go it was small beer compared with our previous actions; like taking a sledgehammer to crack a nut. But as my tank made its way back through the orchard, I experienced the thrill of capturing a German soldier personally. I wouldn't say it was an heroic deed; but, for the record, it happened this way.

The tank was nearing the hedge when I saw, out of the corner of my eye, a grey-clad figure behind some shrubs with a rifle pointing towards us. I instinctively ducked back down into the hatch to alert Sergeant Ellis, and he ordered Taffy to traverse the turret round in the direction of the shrubbery. The sight of the tank's guns pointing menacingly proved too much for the

Jerry: he promptly emerged from his hideaway, threw down his rifle, put his hands into the air, and cried out, '*Kamerad, Kamerad*' in a very shrill and agitated voice.

The sergeant ordered me out to keep him until the infantry caught up with us, which I welcomed as a heaven-sent opportunity to search him for any loot worth taking. The infantry usually got this privilege! I drew my revolver, jumped down from the tank and advanced warily towards the man, who appeared to be in his early twenties. He was shaking a little as I picked up the rifle and threw it out of harm's way. I pulled down his arms and felt to see if he was wearing a wrist watch. He wasn't, but I found and confiscated a pocket watch and a few francs. He had no rings on his fingers or anything else worth taking. Jerry gave me a wry smile, as though to say tit-for-tat. He knew the form, and would probably have done the same to me had he been in my position.

By now the German had calmed down a bit, and I got the feeling he was pleased that for him the war was over and he was unharmed. I escorted him to the tank, ordered him up, and joined him on the rear, still covering him with my revolver. The tank then moved out of the orchard onto the road, and soon afterwards my prisoner was handed over to the custody of the infantry.

The pocket watch was silver, and had a double-flap rear case with the name W. Brand engraved on the inside flap. I have kept that watch to this day as a souvenir, and it is still in working order. Of all the pocket and wrist watches I acquired in various barter deals, this was the one I cherished above all, for the memories of the encounter that day in a Normandy orchard.

It was a long time before I lived down my crew's jokes about my 'single-handed' capture of an armed enemy soldier - backed up, they remarked, with the firepower of a 75mm gun, two Besa machine guns, five revolvers and some hand grenades. Joe Whelan said the soldier was almost dead of fright before I even got to him! I stifled their comments by offering to buy them all a drink with the looted francs later on, although I couldn't split a watch to share out. That was mine.

That Spandau gunner troubled us a little as our troop advanced towards the River Orne, but he always kept one step ahead of us and presumably crossed the river to join up with the main enemy force on the other side. The whole of 107 Regiment, with the infantry and their anti-tank gun support group, also eventually arrived piecemeal at the river, which was narrow here and flowed along between high ground on both sides. We were now facing the enemy, who had withdrawn to the opposite side and were digging in to form defensive positions. They were given no respite, however: during the night the infantry crossed the river and established a small bridgehead. 107 Regiment were to go in the following morning to expand the bridgehead, supporting the infantry in a last-light attack.

The night was reasonably quiet, with just the odd rat-tat-tat of small arms fire from nervous, trigger-happy Germans. We even managed to get a little sleep between guard duties. Birds still sang the dawn chorus, despite the heavy battles in Normandy, and were an enchanting herald to a bright, sunny morning. It was the lull before the hurricane.

I don't profess to know how these things are arranged: do the three squadron leaders toss for it, or is it just the luck of the draw? Whatever the case, A and C Squadrons were deployed in the bridgehead that morning, to join the infantry and launch an attack later in the day. The tanks of B Squadron, meanwhile, were lined up along the near bank, complementing the fire of the anti-tank guns in their dug-in positions in the area.

Everything seemed to be going according to plan during the day: our crew manned *Buzzard*, and we heard various messages passed between the tank troop commanders and their squadron HQs in the bridgehead on the A-set radio. But we knew something was wrong when, as the sun was setting low on the horizon, the near side of the river was peppered with smoke bombs. The familiar whine as they hurtled through the air told us they were 'moaning minnies' fired by the enemy from their multi-barrel mortars. In a very short time our side of the river was effectively screened off with clouds of white smoke, immediately followed by enemy shelling and mortar bombing in the bridgehead area.

Sergeant Ellis checked the time, thinking we should be just

about to put in an attack against them. As battles go, one side usually attacks and the other defends; but this time, by an odd quirk of fate, both sides launched themselves at each other at precisely the same moment. The Canadians were attacking and advancing down from the north, on the east bank of the River Orne, and the Germans must have decided that our bridgehead would be a thorn in their side.

There were no half measures about their attack: they committed the 12th SS Panzer Grenadier Division, complete with SP guns, plus the Tigers of the 502 Heavy Tank Company. Their obvious intention was to annihilate our forces in the small bridgehead. The enemy had been concentrated, and well concealed, in the forest of Grimbosq, the trees of which extended almost to the village of Grimbosq on the perimeter of the bridgehead.

The battle was joined, with both sides fiercely attacking simultaneously, and the air reverberated with screeching tank shells as armour was engaged in combat. The rasping, tearing, fast bursts of Spandaus and slower bursts of fire from Bren guns echoed across the bridgehead, interspersed with rifle fire as the infantry fought each other at close quarters.

My crew were silent and depressed as we followed the course of the battle on the A-set radio: tank commanders from both squadrons were reporting, in high-pitched shouts, tanks being brewed up or knocked out by Tiger 88s and Panther 75s. There were reports, too, of crews being machine-gunned as they baled out and tried to escape. Then all further communication was ended by the enemy jamming the regiment's radio frequency: I thought initially the oscillation was because we were off net, only realising we were being jammed when I tried to retune. But we'd heard enough to know that the bridgehead forces were taking a hammering, boxed in and fighting with their backs to the river. The red sky of the setting sun behind us was symbolic of the blood being spilled as several hundred of our comrades paid with their lives in the effort to maintain the constricting bridgehead on the opposite side of the Orne.

As darkness fell the sounds of battle subsided somewhat, but the area was pitted here and there with little smouldering fires, presumably from brewed up tanks. The crew of *Buzzard* was on the alert, anticipating that we would be ordered to cross the river soon, and we were right. The order came over loud and clear on the B-set, which wasn't affected by the jamming. After an interval of about ten minutes, which seemed like an hour, the tanks of B Squadron moved off to bolster the remnants of 107 Regiment's Churchills in their defence of the bridgehead.

We moved along the high ground by the light of the moon, follow-my-leader style, and eventually stopped at the top of a sunken road leading down to the river crossing. The troop commanders were called to a briefing by Major Davies, B Squadron's CO. When our troop officer put us in the picture, we were under no illusions as to the gravity of the situation and the dangerous task allotted to us. The enemy must at all costs be prevented from crossing the river and breaking through the line, and we were to cross the river at dawn to assist the heavily depleted bridgehead force in preventing them.

There was nothing for us to do but wait for dawn to herald the start of the operation, so I suggested that we have a brew up - rather inappropriate wording under the circumstances. But tea was made and handed round, and we sat in our positions gulping it down. None of us fancied anything to eat. Conversation was sparse. Like me, the others were probably immersed in their own personal anxieties, and pondering on what lay ahead of us in the confined cauldron of the bridgehead. I thought about Tom. There had been many casualties among the other two squadrons the day before, and the odds were shortening against us both coming through safely. I was glad when I had to busy myself netting in to a different frequency on the A-set to thwart the enemy jamming. It took my mind off things for a while.

At first light on another fine morning B Squadron started to move down the steep, sunken road leading to the river crossing. The first tanks across went up on mines, apparently laid overnight by the enemy to stop reinforcements getting in to the bridgehead. It held us up for a considerable time on the approach road to the crossing, and the delay made us agitated: a

75

column of tanks on a narrow road with steep sides would be a prime target if we were spotted.

One man at least seemed unconcerned, as he stopped with his back up against the side of our tank and nonchalantly scribbled in a notebook. When the sergeant and I engaged him in conversation from our perches in the turret, this intrepid character turned out to be a BBC war correspondent. He told us that he'd tried to cross the river, but came under sniper fire from the enemy. Here was a man endeavouring to enter the lions' den of his own accord! These war correspondents were a brave band, risking their lives in pursuit of news from the front line to transmit to the media back home.

The mined tanks were at last moved out of the way and the column started up again, but shortly afterwards we heard on the A-set that our CO's tank had been hit by an 88mm AP. The following tanks were reported to be meeting fire as soon as they appeared at the top of the exit road in the hamlet of Brieux, and had taken refuge amongst some cottages. I knew Tom was in one of them.

I feared the worst as *Buzzard*'s turn came to cross. On our left was a stone bridge destroyed by the enemy after crossing the river, and a Bailey bridge put up by the REs, but it was deemed too dangerous for us to use the Bailey, so *Buzzard* nosed down the bank and entered the shallow river. Then, by a stroke of fate, we stopped dead in the middle of the Orne. We had shed a track plate and couldn't move. I heard Joe cursing in the front, but there was nothing we could do about it: we couldn't replace a track plate underwater, as snorkels weren't included in the tank's inventory. We just had to wait there until the recovery tank pulled us out and we could repair the track on terra firma.

I'm sure the whole crew joined me in thinking how fortuitous it was to break down just at that time. Any delay, no matter how short, before we had to travel the road up to the bridgehead was more than welcome. As we sat in the immobile tank I saw some rings in the water, as if it were raining. The sun was shining, though, and the occasional plops and rings were evidence of sniper fire. I bobbed down further into the turret at this, only to hear Joe shouting excitedly up to me that he could see Tom coming back down the road.

I popped my head back through the hatch and saw Tom, scampering down by a hedge on the right of the road. He reached the river and started to wade through the waist-high water, then stopped as I shouted down to him from *Buzzard*'s turret. I could see his left hand was bleeding.

'I got hit with a bit of shrapnel. It's bloody suicide to go over the top of the hill, Steve. Major Davies has been wounded – his tank was hit by a Tiger.' Tom had apparently been wounded when he was caught out of his tank relieving himself. His tank had been put out of action, but all the crew baled out safely.

I told him to go round to the opposite side of *Buzzard*, which was shielded from snipers, grabbed a field dressing, and jumped out of the turret to bandage his hand. Fortunately it was a superficial wound, with the blood making it look worse than it was, so my prayers for Tom while he was under fire had been answered. By now some other crew members were making their way back, and Tom joined them in their dash to the relative safety of the echelon in the rear.

Soon afterwards *Buzzard* was pulled out of the river and towed to the side of the approach road by the recovery tank. Our track plate was repaired and we negotiated the crossing successfully before driving up the narrow, sunken road on the other side to join the tanks among the cottages at the top. Anti-tank guns had by this time forced the troublesome Tiger to withdraw, so, under cover of our own smoke bombs, B Squadron's battleworthy tanks sought hull-down positions in the area to form a defensive ring around the vital river exit road.

The enemy launched another counter-attack at midday, but this time we were prepared. The artillery behind us put in some deadly barrages, given pinpoint targets by tank and infantry officers, and each area was saturated with shell fire, forcing the enemy armour to withdraw. After that we stood firm, repelling further attacks with our AP and HE gunfire, and were relieved at nightfall by 147 RAC. We withdrew to rear rally to lick our wounds and prepare for the next battle. Only two B Squadron tanks were still battleworthy in every respect, and one was *Buzzard*. Major Davies was unharmed but some of his crew died from wounds.

Captain D. A. Jamieson of the Norfolk Regiment won a Victoria Cross in the fighting; Major Davies (who was originally recommended for the DSO), Captain Cockcroft and Captain Caton were awarded the Military Cross for their part in the battle, in which the regiment suffered severe casualties to officers, men and tanks.

It had been some fight, but the enemy's desperate action to counter-attack our bridgehead forces ended in failure. The armoured divisions exploited our victory by harrying the enemy, who were forced to withdraw. Their armies became trapped in the Falaise pocket, surrounded by the Allies on three sides, and pulverised by immense fire from the ground and by rocket-firing Typhoon aircraft as they tried to escape through a narrow gap at the mouth of the pocket. The German counter-attack against the Americans at Mortain also failed, and these actions became a turning point in the battle for Normandy.

Recovery of tanks went on throughout the fighting, but the following day the regiment could muster only one squadron of tanks, so the tank brigades were reorganised. 7th and 9th RTR transferred to 34 Brigade, which was redesignated 34 Armoured Brigade. 153 Regiment, being the junior RAC regiment in the new brigade, was disbanded, and a composite squadron joined 107 Regiment to become C Squadron. Back at rear rally, 107 Regiment itself produced a composite squadron from the remnants of the whole regiment. It came under the command of B Squadron's CO, Major D. H. Davies, who took over from Lieutenant-Colonel D. H. D. Courtenay, the CO of 107 Regiment, when he became a casualty on 9 August.

Chapter 8

Breakout in Normandy

After a few days we were on the move again, with Tom back in Punchy Porter's crew as the injury to his hand was not serious. The regiment recrossed the River Orne, using the Bailey bridge this time, and followed the tracks of 147 Regiment RAC. They were now in support of the 15th Scottish Division, pursuing the retreating enemy forces trying to extricate themselves from the Falaise pocket and withdraw across the River Seine, and we were to mop up behind them.

We drove our tanks up the sunken exit road, past the ruins of Brieux and the village of Grimbosq. All around us were burnt-out tank hulks, dotting the crater-pitted earth of the small bridgehead, with numerous low mounds marked by wooden crosses or upturned rifles showing the last resting places of those who had fallen in battle. It was a grim reminder, if any was needed, of the lives sacrificed here just a few days ago. All was peaceful now as we passed through the area, and I silently offered up prayers for their souls.

We travelled southward on a road running almost parallel with the River Orne. It was a lovely day and the countryside was beautiful: from the higher ground we could see the river winding through cornfields, orchards and farms, with cattle grazing peacefully in the meadows. We stopped for a while where the Orne wound into a loop near Thury Harcourt, and from my perch in the turret hatch I beheld a sight for sore eyes: on the far bank two young mademoiselles were cavorting about in the water. The lads were catcalling and foaming at the mouth, and I'm sure there would have been a stampede of sex-starved tank crews if the lasses had been on our side of the river! As it was, the convoy moved on before anyone could no longer resist the urge to go for a swim.

The enemy had succeeded in cutting the Flers - Falaise road, so we had a few minor skirmishes in which out Troop Officer, Lieutenant J. Fothergill, and three tank crew died, before our journey ended in a field a few miles west of Falaise. We were greeted with the news that we were to be granted an extended rest, starting in about a fortnight. Cynics confidently predicted we would be in action again in a day or two, but thankfully they were proved wrong, and for the first time since leaving England we were able to relax and live more like human beings.

Out came the bivouacs, which had been stowed away since we left the field in the Juno beachhead to take part in the battles for Hill 112. We wallowed under hot showers in portable bath tents set up for us: it was worth the constant queuing, as I felt clean for the first time in weeks. We also got white bread in our rations for the first time since we had landed in France - it was like manna from heaven!

The reorganisation of 107 Regiment was completed during this rest period. Lieutenant Colonel Rowe returned again as CO, and we were joined by the men from the disbanded 153 RAC Regiment who were to make up our new C Squadron. A and B Squadrons were brought up to strength with reinforcements to replace casualties. The troop acquired a new officer, a fresh-faced young man in his early twenties: Second Lieutenant J. H. Walker. He was immediately nicknamed Johnny, after the famous whisky.

On 20 August we were sent on an outing to see at first hand the devastation of the German armies trapped in the Falaise pocket. The scenes of carnage were indescribable: we'd heard about the terrible slaughter and destruction, but we never imagined it could be so utterly horrendous. The roads had been bulldozed to clear away the wrecked tanks, motorised transport, pulverised human beings and, to our surprise, hundreds of dead horses used by the Germans in some of their transport units. They must have been scraping the barrel in an effort to conserve fuel, we thought, when we came across the dead beasts. Remains of both humans and

5. Lance-Corporal Steve Dyson, May 1945.

6. 3 Troop, A Squadron, 147 Regiment RAC, Lehre, Germany, July 1945. Steve second from left middle row; Tom front row right.

horses were in a state of decomposition, with limbs scattered and blown apart by explosions.

It must have been hell on earth for the Germans trapped on these roads, trying to extricate themselves through the narrow gap of the pocket while under relentless artillery and Typhoon rocket fire from the Allies on the perimeter. They had been literally slaughtered. No wonder their C-in-C, von Kluge, committed suicide: the disgrace must have been too much for him to bear.

It was a hot, sunny day, and the air was heavy with the stench of death. We covered our faces with scarves to alleviate the dreadful smell - the stink at Hill 112 was like Chanel No 5 in comparison. Among the souvenirs I plucked from the scattered debris was a photograph of a German soldier buried in sand, with only his head and shoulders showing. He wore a forage cap and his head was cupped in his hands. The large mound looked rather like a mock grave, and scratched in the sand on top was the legend *Tobruk Mai 1941*. I wondered if this laughing soldier was now buried in a real grave somewhere nearby.

We saw little groups of Germans burying their dead, and I felt a stirring of compassion as we watched the burial parties going about their grisly work under the supervision of our infantry with rifles and bayonets fixed. But the feeling was short-lived when I thought about my own comrades, buried where they fell on the battlefields. For the unhappy German prisoners of war, there was at least the consolation that they had survived the holocaust and would take no further part in the fighting.

One incident had its comical side. A group of German stragglers approached us, dishevelled, hot and tired, and looking very hungry. They almost begged us to take them prisoner, but we were on a day trip and couldn't be bothered, so we waved them away in the direction of some infantry guarding a large group of POWs. They got the gist of our comments and slunk away, surprised and perplexed at our lack of interest!

Within two days of our excursion, the noose had been pulled tight and the gap was closed. The Canadians and the Poles effectively sealed the pocket when their armoured units linked up, and the Germans who had escaped were shattered and demoralised as they crossed the River Seine. The battle for Normandy had reached its climax with a tremendous Allied victory.

Max Hastings, the distinguished author, journalist and broadcaster, wrote a fine book, *Overlord*, to commemorate the 40th anniversary of D-Day in 1984. It details all aspects of the Normandy campaign: the planning and build-up to the invasion; the battles, tactics and weapons; and accounts by survivors from both sides. Some of my experiences, and a photograph of me standing in front of *Buzzard*, are included in the book. I was proud to be associated with the project.

The day after our trip to the Falaise Pocket the fine spell of hot, sunny weather came to an end. Torrential rain fell like stair rods from the darkened sky, as if to cleanse away the blood, filth and stench. *Buzzard*'s crew sat in the bivouac whilst the rain pelted down noisily on the canvas.

On 24 August Tom and I were instructed to report to the squadron office, a large tent in a field. We were concerned in case the summons portended bad news, but Captain Cockcroft and the CO were in a jocular mood as we were ushered in by the orderly sergeant.

'I've just the job for you twins,' said Cockcroft cheerfully. 'I want you to take *Briton* to the tank repair depot at Villers Bocage tomorrow.' He showed us our route on a map: Tom was to drive and I would be the tank commander. Our enthusiasm was plainly evident as we took in the details of an early start and an overnight stop at the depot. Captain Cockcroft cracked a joke about not losing our way and straying into enemy territory. 'We wouldn't want to lose our twins, now, would we?'

The following morning we took our positions in the battered tank, which had been holed through the front of the turret by an 88mm AP shell on 14 August. The tank hadn't brewed up in the incident, but Lieutenant Fothergill had been killed and other crew members injured. The interior was a mess. I guided Tom out of the field and onto the road using the tank radio IC: I was now in sole command of the Churchill, and it was a great responsibility. There was always the danger of meeting fanatical SS stragglers holed up somewhere.

We headed westward, halting every few miles to get our bearings. It was a lovely day and the countryside looked fresh after the recent heavy rains. Everything went according to plan until we were brought to a halt by a milling crowd of people in the village of D'Oilly. They were laughing, shouting and gesticulating in a frenzied manner: a few clambered up onto the tank, and I was kissed on the cheeks by some of the women. We thought we had better get out to discover what the excitement was about - the war might be over, for all we knew.

We were kissed and patted on the back by the crowd, who were talking excitedly and pointing to the shell hole in the turret. Then a man who spoke a little English, and who identified himself as one of the Maquis, enlightened us: Free French troops had entered Paris, and the capital had been liberated. No wonder Tom and I were feted, as sole representatives of the Allies in that village at such an emotional time. We were wined and dined like kings, as though we alone had liberated France; wine and Calvados flowed freely as we gorged ourselves in a café at the invitation of the locals.

We indulged so much that we were in no fit state to continue our journey, so we stayed in the village café overnight. It was marvellous to be able to sleep in a real bed, offered to us with the compliments of the owner of the premises, for the first time since our last leave in March. The following morning, after declining 'one for the road', I was relieved to find our tank just where we had left it. I was responsible for the tank, and just supposing it had been stolen! But we were able to continue our journey, and arrived at the depot without further incident.

We were sent back to our rally point by jeep, and found a letter from Mum awaiting us. She had enclosed a page from *Picture Post* of 12 August 1944, showing eight photos of *Briton*'s crew engaged in tank maintenance, and bearing the headline 'A tank crew prepares for battle in Normandy'. It was sad that so many of those original crew members were by now killed or wounded.

The word soon got round that 34th Armoured Brigade would be taking part in the coming assault against the Channel port of Le Havre, a heavily fortified position bypassed by our armoured divisions after breaking out of the Seine bridgehead. Le Havre was a long way away, and we assumed we would be moved by the fast tank transporters. Much to our surprise and jubilation, however, we learned we were to travel on our own tracks: slower and less comfortable than going on the TCVs, but more exciting, and we would be able to see more of the towns and countryside as we rolled along at a leisurely pace.

We were totally unprepared for the rapturous reception we received at every village and town on the way. The armoured divisions had gone through like a dose of salts, harrying the retreating Germans, but the huge crowds of French people everywhere on our journey treated the slower-moving Churchill regiments as their liberators. We were brought to a halt on many occasions, at which the people took the opportunity to climb on our tanks to hug and kiss us individually. Kisses on both cheeks were welcomed from the young madames and mademoiselles, but a little embarrassing from the monsieurs! We were showered with gifts of wine, fruit and flowers all the way to our first stop, just outside Rouen. We, in turn, gave sweets and chocolate to the excitable children, who ran alongside the moving tanks screaming the only phrase they knew: 'Chocolat, cigarette, pour papa!'. Cigarettes were reserved for the adults.

We enjoyed the ride immensely, travelling through some beautiful countryside before crossing the Seine over one of the damaged and patched-up bridges near Rouen cathedral. The people of Rouen gave us a fantastic and tumultuous reception, with constant stops caused by cheering throngs lining the streets before we eventually harboured a little way out of the city. To our great delight, all those not on guard duty that night were allowed to go into Rouen - a little play before the coming battle for Le Havre. We had earned it: it was the first time we'd been let loose to enjoy ourselves since landing on the Normandy beaches.

All our pent-up emotions were released that night, in a wild fling of wine, women and song. Some of the lads made a beeline for the brothels in the red light district, but the more reverent amongst us, including Tom and I, Bill Powland, the two Jocks, Punchy and 'digger' Digweed, admired the cathedral for a while before finding a café with a piano in it. Tom got tinkling on the ivories, and soon the place was bursting at the seams with lads lured in by the raucous and inebriated singing. A couple of resident whores were doing a good trade, judging by the number of times they disappeared with a customer through the curtains at the rear of the cafe. Our little crowd were more interested in booze, though, and we had one hell of a good time.

The little man with a hammer was working overtime in my head the following morning. Joe Whelan, who had been on guard duty, had a job waking me and the rest of our crew when he came off duty. Thoughtful lad that he was, he brewed up some tea before disturbing us and the hot drink was like nectar. It helped to lubricate my throat and alleviate the soreness caused by all our singing and shouting in the café the night before. My tongue felt like a rasp, for which I blamed the cognac.

The welfare officer had procured tickets for a dance to be held that evening the other side of the city, across the Seine, and a number of us, including Tom and I, decided to go. We travelled there by lorry, and the driver obviously found it difficult to negotiate obstacles in the damaged road. As we were crossing a particularly hazardous bridge, the driver suddenly braked hard in front of a large hole through which you could see the water below. We were all thrown forward into a heap, and as Tom fell he tore his upper lip open on a jagged piece of metal caused by shrapnel or bullets at some time or another.

It was a nasty injury and he was covered in blood, so we bandaged him up as best we could with first aid dressings and dropped him off at a casualty reception station on the other side of the river. Tom was examined by a medical orderly and then detained for hospital treatment, which made me feel very dejected. Poor Tom! His front two top teeth had been knocked out and his mouth was in a frightful mess. The only consolation was that he wouldn't be lining up to take his place with us in the coming battle for Le Havre. The hand of fate!

Next morning we got the order to move on westward towards Le Havre. We were under no illusions as to the enormity of the task confronting us: Hitler would have exhorted his troops to fight to the last man in defence of this vital Channel port. Monty was equally determined to capture the town, to shorten supply lines to his rapidly advancing armies in north-west France and Belgium. The Supreme Commander-in-Chief of the Allied Armies was General Eisenhower, so Monty was free to concentrate solely on planning operations for 21st Army Group, comprising the Second British Army, commanded by General Dempsey, and the First Canadian Army under the command of General Crerar.

The immediate strategy was to capture the Channel ports and V1 rocket launching sites bypassed by the armoured divisions as they pursued the retreating Germans. After that the enemy must be cleared from the approaches to Antwerp, so the port could be used to supply our armies in future operations in Holland and Germany.

We finally harboured in a field outside a village a few miles from Le Havre. Our journey had taken us through pretty countryside, but I was already beginning to miss my twin and our usual get-together on arriving at a new camp. Preparations began for the impending assault: tanks were thoroughly serviced; ammunition checked; guns cleaned and oiled. Then it was just a case of preparing ourselves for the imminent battle. The Church of England padre organised a prayer meeting to help the men, asking for strength and courage in our confrontation with the enemy. It ended with a couple of hymns, in which everyone joined with great gusto. Even the Roman Catholics, such as Joe Whelan and I, attended the ceremony. We knew the Lord would understand, and turn a blind eye to this indiscretion under the circumstances.

Our squadron leader and troop commanders recced the terrain in our line of advance next day, and we were given a briefing on the operation. It did nothing to allay our fears of a hard slog against an enemy well dug-in behind well-prepared defences. Our attacking sector was on the eastern outskirts of the town, so Johnny Walker briefed our troop on the location of all the hazards barring our way: minefields, anti-tank ditches, barbed wire, concrete pill-boxes and dug-outs, anti-tank and field guns, and Spandau machine-gun pits. Hitler had designated the Channel ports as fortresses, and his orders had been followed to the full here in Le Havre. The garrison was estimated to be in excess of ten thousand men, with orders from their Führer to fight to the last man. Would they obey him?

34 Armoured Brigade was disposed, with 107 RAC supporting 147 Infantry Brigade, and 7th and 9th RTRs supporting 56 and 146 Infantry Brigades respectively. The breaching teams would be the Funnies from 79th Armoured Division, including AVREs of the Royal Engineers assault squadrons with bridging aids and fascines. We also had flamethrowing Crocodile Churchills of 141 RAC, and flailing Crab tanks of 22nd Dragoons and the Lothians.

The tanks of 107 Regiment lined up with our infantry on the start line on 10 September. It was a beautiful, sunny Sunday. Although the battles in Normandy had been bloody and hard-fought, at least the enemy had room to retreat when the going got tough. Here, though, the Germans had only the sea behind them: they had a choice of fighting to the finish or ignominious surrender.

We stood around the tank in the late afternoon, smoking and talking, when the peace was shattered by a tremendous roar as wave after wave of bombers passed, dropping their bombs on the town. We could hear the explosions in the distance, and see smoke billowing up from fires here and there. It was reminiscent of the air attack on Caen, and we felt sorry for the poor civilians, but the bombing was essential to make our task a little less difficult. Hardly had the last wave of bombers finished dropping their deadly cargo than a tremendous artillery barrage opened up against the enemy defensive positions. The softening-up action continued for about an hour before the breaching teams of Funnies went into action, to clear pathways through the enemy defensive system ready for the infantry/tank assault.

The clearing operation involved flailing a way through the minefields, laying fascines to fill in anti-tank ditches, and battering concrete pill-boxes with Petard bombs from the Churchills. The enemy were driven out of their strongpoints by flamethrowing Crocodiles. We could hear the noise of explosions reverberating through the night air, and small arms, machine-gun and anti-tank gun fire carried on until well after dusk. The glow from the fires left in the wake of the bombing raid could be seen for miles around.

We spent the night fitfully dozing in turns in our tanks, but dawn brought more activity. The sounds of battle were quite clear, and we could tell from the familiar staccato bursts of machine-gun fire, mingled with explosive shell fire from tank and anti-tank guns, that the infantry/tank operation was under way. We were put on alert to move off at a moment's notice, and bemoaned the fact that the German garrison commander apparently intended to fight it out. Assault forces would now have to battle their way through the outer defences and capture the town, and many lives would be lost unnecessarily.

The order to start the tanks rolling lifted the tension of waiting. Although we'd notched up a few battles by now, we all still felt the usual collywobbles before the off; but once we were on the move and busy with the job in hand, all nervousness disappeared. Our troop advanced warily with the infantry for about a mile before encountering enemy opposition. We drove through a minefield, which had recently been flailed to clear a pathway for our tanks, so the earth was churned up and pitted with small craters where mines had been activated.

As my troop emerged from the safe area, marked on either side with white tape, we came under intense enemy fire. They were obviously expecting us. Our infantry immediately threw themselves down under cover, but I saw one unfortunate lad rear up with the impact of lead and fall forward to the ground still clutching his rifle, then half roll over on his side and lie still. We were at the bottom of a gentle slope, and the quick burpings of a Spandau had our infantry pinned down until plans could be formulated to deal with the menace.

For the first time, I saw the external telephone on the tank intercom being used on the battlefield: an infantry officer crawled round to the rear of our troop leader's tank, took the telephone from the little compartment in which it was housed and spoke to the tank commander. I felt sure Johnny Walker was as surprised to receive the call as I was at seeing the phone used for its intended purpose - more often than not our troop leaders got out of their

88

tanks to liaise with infantry commanders on the ground, or the infantry officers would shout up their instructions or requests from the ground, or jump up on the tank to speak to the commander face to face.

The infantry had apparently ascertained the location of the Spandau position, in a house about half a mile away on our right, and we were asked to put it out of action. It was as easy as shelling peas, with no anti-tank gun and only machine-gun and rifle fire coming from the place. Johnny ordered a set piece attack and off we went, under cover of a bit of smoke. We fanned out through a few hedges, then closed in with rapid fire from Besa guns in short bursts until the infantry lads raided the house to winkle out the enemy. There were a few shots, and shortly afterwards our infantry emerged with two enemy soldiers, one limping badly from a wound. The handful of Germans left in the house were already corpses. After the infantry had signalled the all clear, we opened our hatches to let the cordite fumes out and allow some fresh air in.

It was also an opportunity to have a smoke. I gave one of my cigarettes to Sergeant Ellis, put another in my mouth, and we lit up. Taffy, who preferred rolling his own, was busy doing just that. When he had rolled to his satisfaction and licked the paper, I gave him a light; he took a few puffs, inhaled the strong tobacco, and sat back on his seat. Taffy was never happier than when his finger was on the trigger, and still had an imprint around his eye from the rubber cushion ring of the gun sight on the co-axial Besa. He had a self-satisfied look on his face, from shooting well done. The strong smell of the smoke from his Nosegay tobacco was an antidote in itself to the smell of cordite in the turret, and the singing lilt of his Welsh accent became more pronounced as he enthused excitedly about the recent action.

We waited while the infantry searched the area in the vicinity of the German position, and saw them bring in some prisoners - they had presumably surrendered, judging by the white handkerchiefs they were holding aloft. Meanwhile, looking through the sergeant's binoculars, I could see another troop advancing with their infantry up the slope and disappearing over the ridge, and from the familiar loud cracks of exploding anti-tank gun shells, and Spandau and rifle fire coming from the other side of the ridge, it seemed the troop had run into trouble. A request came over the A-set almost immediately for us to go to their aid.

We advanced straight up the slope leading from the house, getting some cover from a hedge on our left for part of the way, before stopping in the shelter of a barn. Plans were made for our troop and infantry to deal with the anti-tank gun, while the other troop took out the Spandau pit and a concrete pill-box. They had to cross an anti-tank ditch over fascines laid by a breaching tank before they could attack, so we put down a smoke-screen between ourselves and the anti-tank gun while they did so. They went for the enemy positions with guns blazing, leaving the infantry to winkle the enemy out from the pill-box and machine-gun nest. We closed in on the anti-tank gun: Taffy fired an HE and I put another one in the breech, but we were told over the B-set to hold our fire before we used the second shell. As the smoke cleared we could see a white flag being waved to and fro from within the dug-in gun position, so our infantry took over and escorted the prisoners away.

Another two troops leapfrogged us to carry on with the advance, while we had a rest and waited for the half-track to arrive and replenish our ammunition and petrol. It was a good opportunity to make a nice cuppa and enjoy a quiet smoke. Perhaps I should say a relaxing smoke, as it was far from quiet: the noise of battle had reached a crescendo as the outer crust of the enemy was crumbling under our combined infantry/tank assault. We could also hear terrific explosions coming from the town, and we guessed the Germans were blowing up the dock facilities to deny us immediate use of the port. This seemed to be a good omen: they might be considering capitulation, but not before making a mess of the docks.

The enemy soldiers manning the outer defences may also have felt there was little point in fighting or dying for a lost cause if the garrison commander was going to capitulate, because we met only token resistance from the Germans as the tank troops leapfrogged into attack, firing a mixture of HE shells and machine guns. Our infantry brought the enemy in from their pill-boxes, trenches and concrete blockhouses in droves. They looked as if they'd had enough and were glad it was all over. Huge craters everywhere, made during the softening-up process, showed the intensity of the bombing they had undergone; along with our artillery bombardment, the air attack without a shadow of doubt helped the assault forces to achieve their objectives with the minimum of casualties. The Royal Navy also played their part, with two warships firing big guns at enemy gun emplacements. Thanks to these combined efforts, total casualties in capturing the stronghold of Le Havre were reported to be less than 400 men.

It was all over on the following day, 12 September, when the garrison commander, Colonel Wildemuth, surrendered to Lieutenant Bland, a troop leader of 7 RTR. Most of the defenders had already given up, but Wildemuth's action made the capitulation official. There were extraordinary scenes in the town when the exuberant French civilians came out to welcome the liberators and, in some places, inadvertently got caught up in the fighting. The French Resistance assisted in winkling out many German defenders from their hiding places in the town, and also rounded up a lot of French collaborators. They weren't too gentle about it either, in some of the incidents we witnessed. As battles go it couldn't be compared in any way to the ferocious and bloody fighting we'd seen around Hill 112, but it was another one under our belts on the way to Berlin.

As soon as the show was over our regiment pulled out of the town and returned to harbour, wondering if we would be called upon to take part in another assault against a Channel port further up the coast. Imagine our surprise and delight, then, when we were told we were to have an unexpected rest. The brigade's first line wheeled transport was to be commandeered: Allied spearheads had advanced rapidly, causing problems with extended lines of supply from the Normandy beaches, so everything on wheels was needed to assist in the transportation of supplies; and without our transport we were effectively immobilised.

The regiment moved off the next day and travelled for a considerable distance further up the coast, north of Le Havre, then eastward to our destination in a delightful part of the country near Bosc-le-Hard. We settled ourselves in quite happily for what turned out to be a stay of almost two weeks. Our squadron was provided with sleeping quarters in farm buildings, giving us a roof over our heads for the first time since we landed in France, and with a little ingenuity we made ourselves quite comfortable. Before our transport left we all mucked in to unload their cargoes of petrol, ammunition and stores to await their return.

One of the trucks was detained by a day to transport some gear to regimental HQ, and the lorry driver, Frank, had to take along a tank crew trooper to assist him. It goes against the grain to volunteer for anything, but I did in this instance: a little nudge and wink from Frank convinced me that I should go – much to the astonishment of my crewmates, who knew I was very much backward in coming forward as far as volunteering was concerned!

'What's so interesting that you gave me the nod?' I asked Frank as we walked towards his three tonner.

'We're going on a trip to Fécamp,' he replied.

'Is that where RHQ is, then?'

'No,' he replied. 'But it's where the Benedictine comes from.'

I was none the wiser. The only thing I knew about Fécamp was that it had a radio station, because I'd seen the name on the tuning band of our Ekco radio set at home. Frank enlightened me about Benedictine monks and monasteries, in which the former distil a fine liqueur. So it was that, after dumping our load at RHQ, Frank made a long detour through the lovely countryside and finished up at Fcamp. We had no trouble at all in persuading the distillery to trade some bottles of Benedictine for a few jerrycans of petrol which Frank had accidentally left under a tarpaulin while unloading the fuel truck. The war could have been a million miles away as we sat on a clifftop gazing out over the English Channel, and opened up a bottle of the liqueur. Frank took a swig and handed the bottle to me. It was the first time I'd had Benedictine, so I made a wish before drinking: that Tom would be coming back to rejoin the squadron soon.

What with the cognac we'd drunk in the café and now swigs of Benedictine, my imagination ran riot. England seemed tantalisingly close, just across the Channel, and we fantasised about stealing a fishing boat and sailing back home. It was a good day, but on the way back to our squadron we had a near miss when Frank nodded off at the wheel and the lorry careered off the road. We were fortunate to get away with barely grazing the bark off a tree, but my crew enjoyed the story along with some Benedictine round the camp fire that night.

My Benedictine wish was granted the day after the airborne drop at Arnhem: Tom returned cheerfully, but with a clearly visible scar on his face, and a denture to replace his broken top teeth. A couple of days later he received news that knocked the bottom out of his world. I happened to be with Tom when the post was handed out and, as usual when one of us got a letter and the other did not, we shared the news from home. Tom opened his letter, and exploded with excitement: his wife, Rosie, was pregnant. Then I saw his face blanch and assume a malicious expression.

'The bloody cow! It can't be mine! I'll kill her!'

I could scarcely believe it, but he was right. According to the date Rosie gave for the prospective birth of the child, it was as plain as a pikestaff that Tom couldn't possibly be the father. As many thousands of other servicemen had discovered to their horror, Tom's wife had been unfaithful. If infidelity resulted in an unwanted pregnancy, the wives had to face the inevitable consequence when it was crystal clear that the husband wasn't around at the time of conception.

For Tom his marriage ended, there and then. After his rage had subsided he sought advice from his troop officer, who said he would arrange for Tom to see the welfare officer. But, due to the recent reorganisation, B Squadron had no welfare officer at that time, so our CO made arrangements for Tom to see Lieutenant John Foley, the newly-appointed Welfare Officer of A Squadron. Tom was John's first client; while for Tom himself it was the first step on the way to divorce proceedings. His divorce was finalised in court after the end of the war.

During our rest Sergeant Ellis was transferred to RHQ; our troop corporal, 'Brad' Bradley, was promoted to lance-sergeant;

and *Buzzard* was given a new commander, Corporal Bob Bolton. He was a dour, stocky Mancunian, and settled in nicely with the rest of the crew, but we were sorry to see Frank Ellis go. We'd been through many battles with him in command of *Buzzard*, and our crew relied on his judgement: we just hoped Bob would come up to his standard in the battles ahead.

Chapter 9

The Arnhem Corridor

We were rather pleased when news came through towards the end of our rest period that we were to be on the move again, as we didn't want to get rusty. We'd listened avidly on our tank radios to reports of parachute drops by US and British troops to seize the bridges at Grave, Nijmegen and Arnhem. Things were going terribly awry there, and our red beret lads were fighting against overwhelming odds, with the men in the Arnhem corridor thwarted by heavily-reinforced enemy forces from their objective of joining up with airborne troops in the bridgehead.

We guessed we would be required to join in the fray soon, and we were right: Johnny Walker could hardly contain his excitement as he rushed back to our troop after a briefing with the CO one afternoon.

'You can start your packing, lads,' he said, with what looked like a smile of satisfaction at the termination of our enforced rest. 'We're off tomorrow morning to the Arnhem corridor.'

We were almost as excited as Johnny; we'd begun to get a little bored with the rest routine of little to do and plenty of time in which to do it. We were even more delighted to be told we were going on our tracks through France to the Belgian border, and then being taken on tank transporters for most of the way to our destination. But, still minus transport, we had to load the tanks with all our stores and ammunition.

Early next morning - 29 September, my birthday - we set off, with the tanks looking spick and span after the attention they'd received during our layoff, and were again mobbed by rejoicing locals as we passed through the towns and villages. At one stop, in the grounds of an old chateau, we came across a long metal contraption of iron angles and tubes, all buckled up. The recce officer, Captain McKenna, knew what it was: a launching pad for V1 doodlebugs. The Germans billeted at the chateau had obviously done their best to destroy it before making a hurried exit, and we made our own symbolic gesture of retaliation: we pissed on it!

Our journey took us over the River Somme, and I wondered where the Battle of the Somme had been fought during the Great War. My father had taken part in it, and was captured by the Germans there. We passed through many places which had become household names between 1914 and 1918.

When we crossed the Belgian border the crowds seemed even more enthusiastic in their welcome, and we were brought to an enforced halt on many occasions before order was restored by an officer in a scout car. The crews lapped it all up, of course, and accepted the little gifts proferred by the civilians and kisses from the girls with much gratitude and reciprocation.

Eventually, on 2 October, we reached the point where the massive 64-wheeled transporters were patiently waiting for us. It had been a tiring and dusty run for our tank drivers, and Joe Whelan heaved a sigh of relief as he parked *Buzzard* on the transporter and emerged from the driver's hatch. There was time for a rest before we continued on our way, and we washed our compo rations down with wine we had been given along the way. We travelled during the night: it was beginning to get cold after dark, and we were glad of our warm tank suits and abundant knitted woollens. We wrapped ourselves up well and soon snores could be heard from my crew, induced by a smooth ride on the huge rubber-tyred wheels of our host transporter.

At first light we were passing through the streets of Brussels. It was a clear, crisp, early autumn morning, and we were agog at our first glimpse of a continental capital city. The transporters slowed down on entering the outer suburbs, and we had time to get a good look at our surroundings. We were more like a lot of excited schoolboys than tank crews as we looked for famous sights, such as the Manikin Pis. 'There he is,' said Owen, pointing at Taffy. 'He pissed right over the top of that launching ramp!'

The convoy rolled on through almost deserted streets, with just a few early workers on cycles, and the odd pedestrian here and there.

'Look!' shouted Taffy, as we passed an imposing building. 'That must be the Royal Palace.' We argued with him - how could he possibly know? Bob Bolton settled the dispute. 'That's King Leopold's pad, all right. I've seen a picture postcard of it.' The transporters took us just across the Dutch border, via a bridge over the Albert Canal, before coming to a halt. It had been a long ride, all the way through Belgium, and it was time to get our tanks on the road again for the rest of the journey.

A remarkable sight met our gaze as we arrived: the squadron travelling ahead of us were about to move off, and all the crews were smoking long cigars. We knew they wouldn't have bought them, so where did they get them? It didn't take us long to find out; there was apparently a cigar factory just along the road, and the Dutch proprietor was handing out cigars and cheroots to all and sundry. There was a mad stampede to the factory as the news quickly filtered down the line, with tank crews and transporter drivers running pell-mell along the road jostling one another in their haste. They couldn't have been quicker if the bulls of Pamplona had been on their tails: it might be first come, first served, with a limit to the benevolence.

We needn't have worried. The factory owner, a jovial and rather stout Dutchman, had worked out a system while dealing with the rabble of the two preceding squadrons. In broken English he instructed the lads to form a queue; pandering to rank, he waited until the officers sauntering along in our wake arrived and took them in first. They emerged smiling, each clasping a box of cigars. Then it was our turn, and we filed in to be given a choice between a box of cigars or cheroots as a free gift. It was the Dutchman's way of showing gratitude for the 'British liberators', he said, adding his sympathy for our gallant airborne army fighting such a grim battle for Arnhem.

The Arnhem bridgehead was suffering terrible casualties, and our forces in the corridor had been unable to link up with them. With their supplies running out, the 1st Airborne Division were forced to withdraw to the south bank of the Rhine. 107 RAC was still required to help keep open the corridor, now under intense German attack in an attempt to cut off and isolate our forces.

So, amidst clouds of aromatic cigar smoke, we got our tanks on the road again and headed north, trying out Winston Churchill impersonations as we went. We were now well and truly in flat Dutch landscape, surrounded by waterways, dykes and windmills, with spick and span multi-coloured painted houses. It looked a clean and tidy place, and the Dutch people were vociferous in their welcome as the convoy rolled on. We were surprised to find that quite a lot of them could hold a conversation in passable English, and this made our journey more interesting for the lads.

The end of our marathon cross-country trek came as we entered Eindhoven just before dusk. We halted in a side street near a huge factory, which we later understood to be the Phillips complex, and were ordered to dismount and prepare to stay overnight. That meant either kipping inside the tank, or putting up the bivouac and sleeping on the hard pavement. But the friendly citizens were aghast at the prospect. Each tank had its little crowd of curious onlookers, both adults and children, watching our preparations for sleeping.

'Voss iss diss?' asked a plump and red-faced Dutchwoman among the little congregation around *Buzzard*, as the crew erected the bivouac. A look of consternation, if not horror, crossed her rosy features as we explained the object of the manoeuvre, giving a head-on-pillow charade and a few snores to help her understand. She understood all right: after exploding in a torrent of Dutch, and stamping her shoe hard on the pavement while shaking her head a few times, she ran off. A young lad explained to us, in halting English, that she had said the brave English tank men would sleep on the hard stone pavement over her dead body. She would find a bed for every man. I think she must have been a member of the Dutch equivalent of the British WVS, judging by the subsequent way she organised the neighbouring housewives to offer us a bed in their homes.

Clean and fresh-looking women, some with husbands and children in tow, descended on the tank crews to invite us into their homes. Tom and Punchy Porter, who had joined me for a chat, accepted an invitation for the three of us to stay in one house. We were shepherded away by a middle-aged couple, and taken to as neat a little house as I'd ever seen. It was absolutely spotless inside and out, including the clean white bed-linen.

When our hosts discovered that Tom and I were twins, they offered us their own double bed. They would sleep downstairs, they told us in sign language, the husband in an armchair and his wife on the settee. Punchy would have a single bed in another upstairs room. Their teenage boy and girl would share the girl's bedroom, with the boy on the floor. They would brook no argument about the sleeping arrangements, and that was that.

We settled down to what proved to be our most comfortable and pleasant evening since first landing on the Normandy beaches. Out came the best china for a lovely meal, despite the shortages they were suffering. Even tea was supplied, although it was scarce in Holland: the lady produced a packet from a hiding place, surprising even her husband. She apologised if the tea was weak, as she poured it out, explaining in broken English that she was out of practice.

We spent the evening swapping yarns: they were thrilled to find they had three real Londoners in their home, and wanted to know all about the blitz in the East End. We also told them about the doodlebugs - in a recent letter, Mum told me one had dropped on the London Hospital in Whitechapel Road, and I explained to our hosts that my home was only a short distance away as the crow flies - and described Hitler's latest secret weapon, the V2, which dropped out of the blue with no warning noise. They in turn told us of the trials and tribulations of four years under German occupation, living in fear of the Gestapo at all times, with local Jewish people being taken away and never seen again.

It wasn't all gloomy stuff, though, as we had plenty of funny tales to tell of hilarious incidents since landing in Normandy. The time passed quickly, and we finished off a bottle of schnapps the man opened before retiring to our beautiful, soft beds. Our hostess had a bit of a job waking us up in the morning! We plied her with food from our composite rations before leaving, giving cigars and cigarettes to our host, and sweets and chocolate to the children. Then, after a terrific send-off, we travelled north on our tracks to take part in the defence of the Arnhem corridor.

After about four miles we crossed the Wilhelmina Canal, then stopped a mile further on at a place called Son. We kept our eyes and ears open, as there had been recent sporadic enemy attacks from both sides of the road. Standing by on alert, our troop was showered with food, fruit and drink by a charming family: the man, named Johan Van Dinter, gave me his address and hoped we might go back there after the war.

For the next seven days our regiment patrolled the area between Son and Veghel, a vital town about seven miles away which must be defended against any enemy attacks. We saw plenty of gliders in the fields, left after landing the 101 US Airborne Division on 17 September to take the Eindhoven – Grave road at the start of the Arnhem operation. Some gliders had been completely wrecked on landing, and we doubted if their occupants could have survived the terrific crash.

We had a few minor skirmishes with the enemy, in which a bit of Besa fire saw them off, and one sustained attack in a wooded area near St Oedenrode. Meanwhile, news filtered down from the Nijmegen tip of the corridor about how skilfully our forces had withdrawn from the bridgehead to the south bank of the Rhine. They had fought an heroic battle against all the odds, but had been forced to retreat, and the battle for Arnhem was lost. Monty's big gamble had failed. If it had been successful, the war in Europe could have been over by Christmas.

Following our stint in the Arnhem corridor, we moved westward on Monday 14 October and went into harbour at a place called Gierle just outside Antwerp. Rumours abounded: some heard that we were to fight our way along the Scheldt isthmus towards Beveland; others that we were to take part in a northward thrust towards Tilburg. In the meantime, however, we enjoyed another rest period, sampling the delights of Antwerp.

It was hard to believe it had been under German occupation

until a few weeks before: there were few shortages in the shops, and restaurants and cafés were well patronised. The cinemas were packed, and here lay tragedy for some lads from our regiment, who were among the casualties in a cinema that suffered a direct hit from a V2 rocket. They had survived all the battles since we landed in France, and then were killed whilst watching a film.

Our night out in Rouen was like a Sunday school party compared to the sprees we went on in Antwerp. Tom had been a married man in Rouen; now he considered himself parted from his wife pending a divorce, and went to great efforts to put the trauma of her unfaithfulness behind him.

Chapter 10

Fighting with Clarkeforce

Our high life in Antwerp came to an abrupt end when the regiment came under orders again. We were to take part in an operation to clear the enemy from a large pocket west of the Nijmegen corridor.

Our part in the operation would go against all the instructions in tank warfare manuals for infantry/tank operations: our Churchills were to be used for the first time as an exploitation force, a role usually reserved for armoured divisions. This exploitation force, named Clarkeforce as it came under the command of Brigadier Clarke, CO of 34th Armoured Brigade, was to pour through the gap to be punched in the enemy line. In addition to our tanks, Clarkeforce had recce troops, Crocodile flamethrowers, Achilles tank destroyers, infantry and engineers.

In the little town of St Leonard, 20 October dawned bright and clear, with quite a frost about, and any lingering hangovers from our binges in Antwerp were dispelled by an issue of strong rum dished out as we stood by in our tanks. It was the army way of giving us a bit of Dutch courage, and when Johnny Walker briefed us we knew why. The enemy was expected to resist our advance with great determination, with infantry in strongpoints supported by SP anti-tank guns.

Tom, once again, would be missing this party. He was back in the echelon with other spare crew members, not having been assigned to a troop since his return to the squadron after his hospitalisation.

We could hear sounds of the battle going on at the village of

Stapeljelle, a short distance along the road from our assembly point, and we waited rather nervously for the order to move. Our sister regiment, 9th RTR, with their infantry, were attacking to punch through the enemy line and create a gap for Clarkeforce. They seemed to be meeting stiff resistance: we expected to be on our way through the hole in the defences some time during the morning, but in the event it was mid-afternoon before we received the order to start. It was a long wait, and we could have done with another issue of rum.

Johnny Walker led the advance, while Bob Bolton and I followed with our heads and shoulders sticking out of *Buzzard*'s turret hatch. We had a good view of the signs of the recent battle about a mile north of St Leonard: ruined houses, knocked-out tanks and wrecked Bren gun carriers showed the price paid to force an opening in the line. The enemy had evidently suffered too, before being forced to withdraw from the area. We fanned out, with the recce units in front and our infantry in tow, split up into little groups to hunt down and engage the enemy.

Our troop edged forward cautiously across the flat terrain, through farms and narrow lanes, keeping a wary eye open for any lurking enemy amongst the farm buildings. It was a slow process, taking us an hour to travel only a mile. We hadn't seen any sign of the enemy yet, although the sounds of firing on either side of us proved that others were engaging in combat.

Then we heard news that proved fortuitous for Clarkeforce: a bridge near Loenhout had been taken undamaged over a river in our path. This was entirely unexpected, and saved a lot of hard work for the engineers with bridge-laying equipment. Orders came over the A-set for all tank troops to make for the bridge as soon as they cleared their paths of the retreating enemy, who were now denied exit over the river and were gradually being rounded up. The whole regiment crossed the bridge with the infantry shortly afterwards, and plans were made for an assault on our next objective, Wuestwezel.

It was dark by the time the details of the attack were settled, but we still had to go on, despite expressions of astonishment from the drivers. Joe Whelan asked Johnny Walker for a ration of carrots to improve his night vision, and the ragging helped to relieve the tension before the assault began.

The defenders of Wuestwezel evacuated as soon as the first shots were fired by the attacking force and, with the exception of a few tail-enders who weren't quick enough, the bulk of the enemy retreated. We drove through the streets while our infantry searched the houses for any lurking enemy. It was very dark, and in the gloom I could just make out the figures of a few prisoners being pushed along by infantry, looking rather menacing with their fixed bayonets.

After the successful capture of Wuestwezel, we stopped our tanks and began to investigate nearby buildings to find somewhere to sleep. We'd been up well before dawn that morning and were all very tired. *Buzzard*'s crew found a house just a few yards away, and the infantry told us it had been cleared out and was safe to enter.

Bob Bolton went to confer with Johnny Walker, and returned with bad news. 'Don't make yourselves comfortable, lads. We're on the move again.' It was 11.30pm, and we were incredulous. Taffy muttered that our tank had only got this far in the dark by following the lights of the tracer ammunition he'd been firing. Joe had already nodded off, exhausted, and was woken up with the news. He was speechless for a few seconds, then exploded with protests. We returned to our tank to prepare to advance again, and made a strong brew of tea to keep us awake.

Johnny Walker arrived to commiserate with us and explain why it was necessary to push on overnight. The regiment was to attack Nieuwmoer, the next village in the line of our advance, the following morning; and we had to get as near as possible to the village before the enemy could get properly organised after their withdrawal from Wuestwezel. Rain started to pelt down, and we pulled the hoods of our tank suits over our heads as a protection against the driving and lashing deluge. There were grumbles that we would get pneumonia before we got to Nieuwmoer as, drenched and hooded, we made our way through the darkness towards the tanks. It was now about midnight.

Buzzard's crew mounted up and waited for the order to move.

We could hear the small recce tanks as they passed us on their way to the front to head the column. Then we received the order to start up: seldom, if ever, could a little town like Wuestwezel have heard a whole regiment of Churchill tanks start up their engines almost simultaneously. The noise reverberated through the streets, making as much noise as a hundred Lancaster bombers passing overhead. I thought the deafening roar of the engines would be heard in Roosendaal, never mind Pneumonia (the pseudonym our troop had rapidly adopted for Nieuwmoer), and the enemy would be expecting us.

B Squadron followed hard on the heels of A along a narrow country road out of the town. Bob and I were very uncomfortable, heading into the driving rain and keeping our eyes peeled all the time for any eventuality. Joe was cursing the conditions: the darkness and rain made it difficult to keep the front tank in sight and avoid the ditches on both sides of the road. 'It's more of a nightmare than a night march,' he hollered up from the driving compartment. Taffy and Owen both seemed quiet, and I guessed they had nodded off. Their services were not required for the time being, so they could be excused.

We made slow but steady progress in a northerly direction for about two hours, stopping and starting at intervals, with only the rumbling of the tanks and the sound of torrential rain beating down continuously to disturb the night air. Then events up front brought the whole column of tanks to an abrupt halt. Joe stopped *Buzzard* just inches from *Brecon*, the troop sergeant's tank. The reconnaissance tanks had met up with the enemy: we could hear exchanges of fire, and the night was lit up by glowing streaks of tracer ammunition whizzing by around us. We heard on the A-set that the recce troop had come under fire at a roadblock, so we turned off our engines and listened until all went quiet. The enemy had been beaten off by the recce unit.

A Squadron surmounted the road block and drove forward, spraying their Besa fire in all directions just to make sure. They were a few hundred yards in front of us, but the rapid fire of the Besas created quite a din, and the area was lit up again with their tracers. After that all was quiet until the regiment harboured in a nearby field.

We had three hours before the morning stand-to at 06.00, during which the tanks were refuelled, ammunition replenished, and the crew ate some compo rations washed down with a cup of char. Most of us were overtired and couldn't settle down to sleep, however much we tried. We just sat inside our tanks with hatches closed to stop the rain getting in, talking about our assault against Wuestwezel. Our casualties were infinitesimal, which proved we had achieved the surprise our commander intended. But what lay in store for us at Nieuwmoer, now the enemy was alerted to danger and had had time to prepare defences?

The order to stand by ready to move came at 05.45, and another issue of rum was gratefully received to warm us up on this cold and nervous morning. A couple of hours passed before we were given the order to move, third in the advance behind A and C Squadrons. The rain had eased up by then, for which Bob and I were grateful. We passed the site of last night's roadblock, evidenced by the amount of stuff pulled to the sides of the road and a couple of German corpses lying half in a ditch.

Our assessment that the Germans would be well-organized in defence was proved correct: they seemed to have SP guns all over the place. The regiment fanned out on both sides of the road just before Nieuwmoer, with C Squadron fighting through the centre of the village. It was a cut-and-thrust affair, with heavy fighting for the best part of the day before the enemy withdrew.

The worst time for my crew was in mid-morning, skirmishing with an SP gun. Using smoke and troop tactics we raked its position with a mixture of AP and HE 75s, only to find when the smoke had cleared that it had trundled back to another position. We were advancing after one of these episodes when I saw an enemy soldier jump up suddenly, pointing the German equivalent of the British Piat infantry anti-tank weapon, the Panzerfaust, at *Buzzard*. My heart nearly stopped beating but, before I could shout out a warning, I saw the German fall under a hail of lead from one of the troop's machine guns. His Panzerfaust shot ricocheted off the side of *Buzzard*'s turret. The ditch in which he had been hiding was only about 25 yards away, and I am sure that if the gunner hadn't spotted him and mown him down, deflecting his aim just as he fired, the shot would have penetrated our tank. I looked at the statue of the Virgin Mary and offered up prayers for the near miss.

The enemy eventually withdrew from the village, but not before inflicting a lot of casualties on the attacking force and putting a few of our Churchills out of action. While the battle was raging the enemy also endeavoured to cut off the corridor in our rear with an armoured attack north-west of Wuestwezel; but they were beaten back in a day-long engagement by the remainder of 49th Division and 147 RAC of the 34th Armoured Brigade. We felt a little safer when our regiment harboured for the night and we heard the news of this battle.

It was a very cold and wet night, and we looked around for somewhere to sleep under cover, finishing up on the concrete floor of an abattoir. We were so tired, however, that we were oblivious to our surroundings. I must have fallen asleep the moment my head touched the rolled-up overcoat I was using as a pillow.

The regiment continued the advance early next morning, and for the next couple of days Clarkeforce snapped at the heels of the enemy, who were fighting hard as they carried out a skilful withdrawal northwards. Their SP guns would fire at us from well-camouflaged positions, then quickly disappear under cover of a smoke-screen as soon as we got a range of fire at them. It was gratifying to be in at the kill of one of the blighters, which went up in flames after a troop attack in which we used a lot of smoke and fired off a few 75mm AP shots. Taffy claimed our gun had done the damage, but *Briton*'s gunner was convinced he had hit the target. They tossed for it, and Taffy's grin spread from ear to ear as he called correctly: another one up for *Buzzard*.

We fought our way through several hamlets and villages, each engagement bringing its toll of infantry and armour. Part of our regimental echelon in the rear was ambushed and captured, and Regimental Sergeant-Major Gregg was killed - the only death among the casualties. The echelon was later released, but several vehicles were lost.

After four days of continuous advance against a courageous enemy fighting a ruthless rearguard action, we were granted a day for rest and maintenance. The going had been gruelling for both men and machines, and we needed the respite before continuing with the advance. We gave our tanks a thorough overhaul and a good clean-up inside, but the mud and dust was left on exteriors as it formed a useful camouflage. *Buzzard*'s turret now boasted an indentation on the front corner to match the one on the opposite corner caused by the AP hit we sustained at Hill 112. Taffy fingered the indentation and, not for the first time, pointed out that if the shot from the Panzerfaust had been a foot to the left and about six inches down, it would have knocked his head off. Bob Bolton commented drily that, where he was sitting, it would only have castrated him.

The guns having been stripped, cleaned, oiled and reassembled, the engine serviced, and the tracks tightened, the rest of the day was spent in catching up with letter-writing and so on. We always kept an eye open in case of a surprise attack from SP guns, and we were so on the alert during the afternoon that we manned our tanks when we heard a tank engine in the distance, getting louder as it neared us. Bob Bolton looked through his binoculars at the approaching vehicles, and recognised one of our scout cars and a Sherman tank. They came to a halt by our troop, and the Sherman commander shouted out to Johnny Walker to take them to our CO. Johnny hastily climbed onto the Sherman and off they went. The Sherman commander was Brigadier W. S. Clarke, commander of Clarkeforce, and Johnny told us later that the Brigadier was suitably impressed with our alertness to possible danger.

B Squadron was first on the road at 06.00 hours next morning, 26 October, and Clarkeforce continued to advance northwards, encountering only minor hit-and-run skirmishes until we got to Brembosch. The enemy decided to make a determined stand here, with numerous SP guns in well-camouflaged positions blocking the approaches to the village. We also came under heavy shell fire, but Brembosch was eventually cleared of the enemy by the afternoon. Clarkeforce lost a couple of Churchills and one

17-pounder SP gun, although we succeeded in knocking out two German SP guns in return. Sadly our squadron leader, Major Davies, and two of his crew were badly wounded in the attack.

The next two days were the hardest period of the advance, and at dawn on 28 October we came under surprise attack from an enemy SP. The regiment had harboured overnight spread out amongst a group of houses and farm buildings; my troop rested rather uneasily in a barn, awaiting the arrival of the ammunition and fuel trucks to replenish our tanks. The convoy of three tonners arrived just as dawn shed the first light on the morning mist. Our crew joined in with the others unloading ammunition and petrol and taking it back to our tanks, berating the drivers lightheartedly for their failure to reach us the previous night as they should have done. Bill Hollowbread had brought Donk, the SSM, along in the half-track with him.

All hell was let loose while our crew was busy replenishing *Buzzard*. I had finished stowing shells away in the hull bins and was helping Joe fill up the petrol with jerrycans when we were attacked by the SP. We were caught with our pants down! The SP gunman made the most of it while he could, and shots came at us in rapid succession. As the first explosion rent the morning air, Joe and I were of one mind. We had to find cover – but not in the tank, which was an obvious target. We jumped down and followed the rest of the crew into a nearby ditch, feeling as naked as the infantry as we crouched down. We heard further explosions, shouts and screams as the SP hit its targets: the wily enemy had waited for an opportune time before striking, when the echelon trucks had arrived and the crews were out of their steel cocoons busy replenishing the tanks.

Recovering from the initial shock of the surprise attack, our troop raced back to man our tanks, closing the engine hatch covers and waiting for orders from the troop commander. Johnny had been observing the likely site of the SP through his binoculars, and had caught a glimpse of it as it changed firing position. On his order our troop skirted the barn under cover of a bit of smoke and stopped behind a hedge. Johnny pinpointed the spot where the SP had disappeared among some trees, and our three tanks plastered the area with AP shots. Some other tanks were mobile soon afterwards and firing at the SP's last sighting, but we all missed the blighter, as we discovered when we combed the area. The SP crew must have felt like a duck in a shooting gallery, and had beaten a hasty retreat with their gun.

There was no further trouble as the regiment was organised for the attack against Wouw, planned to take place at 08.00 hours. It was delayed a little because of the SP incident, but the regiment eventually moved off, leaving a still-smouldering tank from C Squadron and three burnt-out trucks as a warning to us to be more alert.

Clarkeforce's objective was now to capture Wouw and cut the road leading to Bergen-op-Zoom. 107 Regiment, supporting the infantry, advanced behind a creeping barrage from our artillery. A and C Squadrons carried out a left-flanking attack, while B Squadron took the centre. As the regiment advanced we came under incessant mortar fire from the enemy, which took a toll of the poor infantry lads preceding us as far as the railway embankment. Over the other side of the embankment the tanks took the lead, plus 17-pounder SP guns. The enemy fought tenaciously, but could not prevent the tanks of A and C Squadrons getting astride a vital road and then fighting their way through to the town.

Meanwhile, B Squadron was occupied in advancing with our infantry on the right, firing at any enemy vehicle in sight, until we reached a windmill at one end of the road going through the centre of the town. We followed on the heels of A Squadron, assisting the infantry to clear the enemy out of buildings, and they were soon surrendering piecemeal. It was all over bar the occasional snipers, who were eventually winkled out by the infantry with some covering fire from tank Besa guns, and Clarkeforce was now in possession of Wouw.

Shortly after the battle died down, crowds of exultant Dutch citizens emerged from cellars and other hiding places to greet their liberators. Some of them had already been busy rounding up collaborators and informers, and *Buzzard*'s crew watched as these wretched people were manhandled along by an irate mob to the church in the centre of town. We understood they were to be imprisoned in the crypt for the time being. Later in the evening the enemy sent over an artillery barrage, and the church was one of the buildings reduced to rubble: an HE shell set fire to the steeple and then engulfed the whole church in flames. One could only hope that the captives had been taken away in time, and were not left to perish under the smouldering ruins.

Our regiment harboured in Wouw for the night, having achieved its immediate objective. It was, in fact, the end of Clarkeforce's successful advance. The following day 9th RTR supported the Hallamshires in the attack against Roosendaal, after coming up on the right flank of Clarkeforce. On their right, 147 RAC was in support of the 104th US (Timberwolf) Division, who were having their first taste of battle.

34th Armoured Brigade could justifiably be proud of the end result, and particularly of 107 Regiment spearheading Clarkeforce. We had played our part, with the 4th Canadian Armoured on our left, in capturing Roosendaal and Bergen-op-Zoom and sealing off the South Beveland isthmus. This would enable the British and Canadians to overrun the islands of South Beveland and Walcheren, and the Breskens pocket on the opposite banks of the Scheldt estuary, thus freeing the approaches to the port of Antwerp for use in the ever-mounting supply build-up for the impending battles on German soil.

On 29 October the Clarkeforce units reverted to their normal commands, after advancing 25 miles in ten days of continuous fighting against a determined and tough enemy rearguard. 107 Regiment left Wouw and travelled on its own tracks to the town of Breda, where we were stationed in a large jam factory for a few days' rest. Although the concrete floor was uncomfortable to sleep on, at least there was variety in the different jams we ate on our hard biscuits! Here too all the regiment was together again, and I was reunited with Tom.

Chapter 11

Through the Dutch Defences

Our next move in Holland was to a place called Oudenbosch, where we had it even more jammy for the next three weeks. We stayed at a very large building called The St Aloysius College for The Christian Brothers, The Institute St Louis. We were made welcome by the brothers, who organised all sorts of competitive games between themselves and our troops. They provided facilities for various activities, including football, table tennis and darts.

There was also a theatre, which was a good excuse to put on a stage show. John Foley was given the job of organising a concert party, in which Tom and I participated, and the event turned out to be hilarious. The Squadron Airs also got together during our stay in Oudenbosch, and put on some shows for the lads. The monastery may have been austere, but it was paradise compared to some of the places we'd been recently.

At the end of November another battle was found for 107 Regiment, and we bade a fond farewell to the brothers as they congregated in the grounds to send us off with prayers for our future safety. Tom was now back with Punchy Porter's troop and would once again be taking part in battle with me. We moved to a place called Budel, where the regiment came under command of 31st Tank Brigade for an operation to clear the Germans from their last stronghold on the west side of the River Maas. The town of Blerick, with its formidable defences protecting Venlo on the eastern side of the Maas, was to be assaulted and captured by 44th Brigade with 31st Tank Brigade under command.

7. After the broadcast (see pp 202-5) at 376 Bethnal Green Road. *Standing:* Albert Craske, Dick Bridgen, Bob Dyson, Tom Dyson, Steve Dyson, John Murphy, Bob Dyson Senior; *Seated:* Phyllis Dyson, Maggie Craske, Eileen Dyson; *Kneeling:* Albie Craske.

8. The author revisits Normandy on the 45th anniversary of D. Day.
Above: At Courseulles, near where he came ashore on 1st July, 1944;
Below: At Pegasus Bridge.

B and C Squadrons of 107 RAC were committed, and joined the rest of the attacking force on 31 November to travel to an assembly point at Maasbree. The force was under the command of Brigadier Knight, CO of 31 Tank Brigade, and included flail tanks, bridge-laying Churchills, two squadrons of APCs, and a squadron of Crocodile flamethrowers.

We arrived at the assembly area on 2 December, and at 05.25 hours on 3 December the artillery softening-up process began. The 400 guns of the RA kept up a continuous barrage for over two hours, and the town of Blerick was hidden under a huge pall of smoke from raging fires. It was the largest concentration of guns used on so small a target so far. The area was also plastered by the 1st Canadian rocket projector units, being used for the first time. Each of their six 'mattresses' was capable of discharging 350 rockets simultaneously into an area 200 yards square. We were on stand-by with our tanks that morning, and wondered whether there would be anything left for us to attack after such a terrific bombardment.

The order to advance came at 07.45 and the Churchills of 107 RAC advanced through the cloying mud, providing close covering fire for the flail tanks sweeping the minefields and clearing the wire entanglements. The bridge-laying Churchills were then able to lay pathways over anti-tank ditches, but a couple of our Churchills got bogged down in the mud and had to be pulled clear. At one stage my troop, along with another from B Squadron, was ordered to fire 'pepperpot' shot at a difficult enemy defensive position. Taffy loved it as we joined the other five 75mm guns with rapid fire on the target, and my arm ached with the continuous loading of shells.

It turned out to be a short and sharp battle: by one o'clock in the afternoon the infantry were fighting in the centre of Blerick, and three hours later it was all over. Once again the Churchills and Crocodile flamethrowers had proved their worth against the enemy strongpoints, after the Funnies had breached the defences on the town's perimeter, and 107 RAC casualties were minimal. The town and its garrison were captured and the Dutch citizens emerged from their cellars, a little shell-shocked maybe, but glad to greet their liberators. The enemy had now been eliminated from the Maas pocket.

B and C Squadrons rallied at Maasbree and then moved to Nederweert, where Captain P. E. Tapson took over command of B Squadron. Out came the compo rations, and we sat around chewing over them while discussing the assault. Tom was obviously glad to be back in action for the first time since his accident on the bridge at Rouen, not least because we were fighting together now he was once again part of a tank crew.

The supply trucks arrived, bringing not only ammunition and fuel but also rumours of another impending action for our regiment. This was confirmed when, after an overnight stay in Nederweert, we were moved to Brunssum, in Limburg, to prepare to attack the formidable defences of the much-vaunted Siegfried Line. The regiment settled in to wait for a suitable time to start the operation: the going was considered too muddy for the tanks, and the planners were hoping for a few days of hard frost before embarking on the offensive. We waited and waited for a cold spell, but at least we were found comfortable accommodation by the townsfolk while we did so.

In my memory incidents are associated with names of places, and one extraordinary incident took place at Brunssum. Joe, Owen and I shared a room on the third floor of a block of buildings in a communal square. I returned to the room round about midnight on Saturday 10 December, having just finished my two-hour stint on guard duty with Taffy, and woke up Joe and Owen for their turn on duty. I got into bed as soon as they left, and was almost asleep when I heard the creak of the door slowly opening and the dim landing light spread into the room. The figure of a woman emerged through the doorway and approached my bed. I thought I was dreaming, or that it was a ghost; then realised it was Marie, the woman from the ground floor flat, standing by the bed in her dressing-gown. In the palm of her hand, as she held it out, was a condom.

She didn't utter a word (not that I would have understood the language, anyway), but she didn't have to: her actions had said it all. She wasn't just creeping around at night selling contraceptives;

the sheath was brought along for her own protection. I didn't really fancy her, but at least she was hygienic! On the Sunday morning I saw Marie attend communion at mass in the Catholic Church. She must also have been to confession with the priest beforehand, to beg forgiveness for her indiscretion.

Chapter 12

The Battle of the Bulge

By 16 December the weather still hadn't altered, so plans for the operation involving 34th Armoured Brigade were abandoned in favour of moving us to the Tilburg area to train with the 43rd Division for another operation. The move would be made on tank transporters, which arrived on the morning of 17 December to load the tanks - much to the fascination of Brunssum's inhabitants. The regiment moved off to a rousing farewell from the kind people who had made us so welcome during our stay.

But we never reached our intended destination: a dramatic event altered the course of our journey through the foggy weather. The Germans launched an offensive on a wide front in the Ardennes, and their Panzer divisions broke through the American defence line in several places. We didn't know the reason for our long column of transporters being brought to a halt on a road somewhere in Holland though, so we just sat on our tanks, on top of the transporters, and watched the comings and goings of officers and despatch riders up and down the line.

There was a long wait before Johnny returned to our troop to tell us we were being diverted south. 'The enemy have made a breakthrough in the Ardennes, and we're being sent down to the Americans' sector to be on hand if we're needed quickly.' We were to stop the Germans if they got to the River Meuse, although demolition charges were already in place to blow up the bridges if necessary.

The convoy doubled back on itself, and finished up that evening in the Belgian town of Tongres. We were the object of much curiosity from the few Americans around as we drove into the town, but the people of Tongres gave us a great welcome. They were overjoyed to see British troops in their midst.

Over cognac and cigars in a café that night, with the compliments of some Americans, we learned how serious the situation was. The German attacks had achieved maximum surprise and, as in 1940, their Panzer divisions were pouring through the gaps punched in the Ardennes front line. How was it possible, we thought: weren't the Germans down, if not out?

As the situation was so critical the tank crews had to be within a short distance of their vehicles at all times, which meant finding accommodation in a house with the tank parked outside the front door. *Buzzard*'s crew were adopted by the most wonderful and kindly family you could ever wish to meet: Jean Baar-Bruls, his lovely wife, Anna, and his two young children, Emilleke and Joske. An attractive girl named Guillimine Grommen, known as Mini, was boarding with them at the time. Jean let our crew bed down in the front room for the duration of our stay. The weather turned very cold, and snow arrived in due course, so it was marvellous to be able to sit around a lovely fire and keep warm when we weren't on duty. We used all the facilities in the house, and showed our appreciation by showering the family with stuff from our compo rations.

Our role at Tongres was to mount roadblocks on the roads leading into the town, and monitor incoming traffic. As the days passed it became clear that the Germans had launched a very large-scale offensive, and were aiming to cross the Meuse bridges and drive on to Brussels and Antwerp like a second Dunkirk.

The Americans based in the town, manning anti-aircraft batteries, told us that confusion reigned in their sector because English-speaking Germans had been caught wearing American uniforms and driving jeeps. There were also tales of Germans massacring American prisoners, which served to bring on the jitters. Every American was looked upon with suspicion as a potential wolf in sheep's clothing.

One jeep, with a handful of GIs, failed to produce the required pass and was detained by our troop for further investigation by

American military police. The detainees were subjected to the sort of questions which could only, supposedly, be answered by a true American. We thought we had bagged a prize when the MPs disarmed the GIs and escorted them away under guard; but one MP told us they thought the men might be on the run. 'They've come from Dinant, and say the Germans are just over the other side of the river there. We're taking them in for interrogation.'

This incident did little to assuage our feeling that the British had been sent to pull American chestnuts out of the fire. But our opinion of the fighting qualities of our American allies changed as we began to hear of their defensive battles. At the town of Bastogne the American defenders were beleaguered by German forces, and called upon to surrender. The Germans received a rather perplexing one-word reply from the American commander, Brigadier McAuliffe. 'Nuts.' Our allies could not only fight hard, but also obviously had a terrific sense of humour under adversity! The Americans' stock with us went up again when their anti-aircraft fire hit a German dive-bomber during a bombing raid on Tongres, and sent it hurtling down to earth in flames.

During our stay in the town we had a few impromptu musical evenings at Jean and Anna's house. Tom, Punchy, Bill Powland and Jock Gould would join our troop, Tommy Reilly brought his guitar, and the lads would have a sing-song. Our host family loved the parties, and were tickled pink when I first introduced Tom as my twin. Anna could speak English fluently, and Jean reasonably, but Mini could only manage a little. Mini had a boyfriend, nicknamed 'Happy Sam' because he was constantly moaning about things and always looked miserable.

It was evident from the beginning, however, that Mini took a fancy to me, and as the days went by she made it clear that she would pack up her boyfriend for me. She even asked me to marry her, and take her to London with me when the war was over. You can imagine the ribbing I got from the lads: I was the knight in shining armour for Mimi, the singing troubadour. Anna also told them that Mini had asked me to marry her, which gave Tom and the lads the idea of springing a surprise at a party on Christmas night.

Tom and I, and some of the lads, attended midnight mass at the Church of Our Lady of Tongres on Christmas Eve. It was the sixth Christmas of the war, and the church was packed to the rafters with local civilians and American and British forces. The choir was backed by the American Forces Band, and it was very moving when the whole congregation joined in singing 'Silent Night'. Everybody prayed for an early end to the war.

The party at the Baar–Bruls' home that evening went with a swing: we'd managed to get plenty of beer and cognac, and everyone was in good spirits. I hardly noticed when Jean and Anna left the room with Mini until, to the strains of 'Here Comes the Bride' from Tommy Reilly's guitar, the door opened and in came Jean, dressed to look like a priest, followed by Mini in bridal white lace on Anna's arm. I thought it was some sort of Belgian Christmas party game, and was joining in the uproarious laughter provoked by their entrance, when Tom stepped forward, grabbed my arm, and said, 'Come on, Steve, I'm the best man. You're going to be married to Mini.' Then the penny dropped!

I played my part perfectly as the bridegroom in this charade. Jean conducted the mock wedding ceremony, realistically reading from a book. Mini said 'I do,' as if she really meant it and wished it wasn't all just make-believe. Tom produced the ring, borrowed from Anna, which I put on Mini's finger. 'I now pronounce you man and wife,' intoned Jean. Mini and I kissed and embraced, whilst the lads toasted us with cognac. 'I'm Mini Dyson now,' she giggled, as Tom and the lads kissed the bride. She really did look lovely with her pretty face, outlined by the veil over her dark hair, wreathed in a smile that deepened the dimples in her cheeks. What a pity the mock wedding didn't extend to consummating the marriage.

Next day the Germans were halted and beaten back at Celles, just four or five miles from the bridge over the Meuse at Dinant. The British 29th Armoured Brigade helped the Americans to regain Celles, which proved to be the furthest enemy penetration in the Battle of the Bulge. Our prayers to the Blessed Virgin Mary in the Christmas Eve mass had seemingly been answered.

A few days later orders came from 30th Corps HQ for 34

Armoured Brigade to cross the Meuse and pursue the retreating Germans in the Ardennes. We'd proved good at this sort of thing before in the flat countryside of Holland, but we were in blissful ignorance of the nightmare ahead of us in the snowbound woods and hills of the Ardennes.

We had enjoyed our stay in Tongres, protecting Liège and the Meuse bridges with our blocking positions. It was a wrench to have to leave the people who had welcomed us into their homes and made Christmas so happy and memorable for us all. But our RASC friends arrived with their tank transporters to give us a lift to Dinant, where we were to cross the Meuse, and it was time for tearful final farewells. The people were sad to see us depart: Jean said Tongres could never forget the British soldiers, and would remember us every Christmas for the great joy we brought while we were there.

'You not forget,' said Mini, wiping the tears from her eyes as I kissed her goodbye. 'You marry me for real next time, Stefan. I love you always.' Anna embraced us in turn, and said in her perfect English, 'It was so marvellous to have you in my home. It has been our happiest time since the war started all those years ago. I pray to God to keep you safe and hope you can come back one day to stay with us again.'

The transporters started to move slowly away, with Anna, Mini and the two children waving and keeping pace with us for a while. As we gathered speed Mini ran along until she was forced to stop, waving and blowing kisses which I knew were meant for me alone.

We headed south through spectacular countryside, although it was very cold and we soon sought sanctuary from the elements inside our tanks. The transporters were going at high speed, and sitting on the outside was like being in a wind tunnel. But we didn't go by transporter all the way: after about fifty miles the convoy came to a halt, and the tanks were unloaded to finish the journey on tracks. After the inevitable brew up and smoke we set off, glad to be under our own steam again – we were never too happy with the piggyback method of transport. The transporters were invaluable, though, as a means of transferring tanks from A to B in the shortest possible time; the RASC lads did a really marvellous job, often under the most adverse conditions, and were generally a cheerful lot.

We eventually came in sight of the River Meuse on our left as we drove along the road leading to Dinant. It was in a lovely setting, with a background of trees and buildings on high ground on the opposite bank.

The column of tanks slowed down and almost came to a halt as we approached the bridge at Dinant. Much to my amazement I saw a colonel in the middle of the road, gesticulating like mad to get us over the bridge quickly. We felt honoured, as we were more used to humble redcaps directing the traffic. We later heard that this character was nicknamed the 'Mad Colonel'.

After crossing the Meuse on 29 December our regiment went into harbour at Celles - the town which had seen the furthest penetration of Von Rundstedt's offensive only four days before. Evidence of their recent presence, and the fight by American and British forces to retake the town, lay all around us in the usual post-battle debris.

I came across a German corpse in a wooded area and searched through his pockets, but anything of value had already gone. I did find and take a *Merk Buch 1945*, a German diary for 1945. The poor man hadn't lived to write in anything for *Montag 1 Januar*. Little could he have known when he procured the diary that a British soldier would be filling in the daily events instead of him.

My first entry, on 1 January, records that we were still at Celles; that it was a good day for aircraft; and that I wrote some letters to friends and family. I was sitting at a table in the wrecked Pavillon Ardennais, a restaurant at the main road intersection in Dinant.

The following day the regiment was ordered to move through the Ardennes, attacking the slowly retreating Germans wherever possible. It was the start of a dangerous and gruelling journey. Our tanks slid over the frozen roads like curling stones on ice, and the further we went the worse conditions became. It took us most of that day to get as far as Ciergnon, about four miles away, where we stayed the night; and the punishing journey continued the next morning.

Our tanks got into all sorts of difficulties on the steep climbs over hilly countryside. Downhill descents were extremely hazardous, with the tanks behaving like toboggans, and the drivers were at times unable to retain control. The steel track plates sliding on the icy road surface made steering a hit or miss affair, with more hits than misses as tanks went into crabwise skids, out of control until colliding with something at the roadside or landing in a ditch. All the hazards added hours to the journey, as tanks in difficulties had to be given help, and played havoc with our nerves. The unfortunate drivers had the worst time, while the rest of the crews spent more time out of the vehicles than inside, trying to help the drivers in the most troublesome spots. It was a relief when we got the opportunity to leave the road and go across country, where the tank tracks could get a grip in the ground and we could move along more easily.

That night we stayed at a village called Haversin; again only a few miles further on our way through the snow-covered countryside. We slept anywhere we could find cover: getting shelter was not just the top priority, but essential for survival. We were already halfway to hypothermia after struggling knee-deep through snow all day in near arctic weather conditions. No matter how many extra woollens we wore underneath, we just couldn't get warm. I don't know how I was able to get my tank suit on over sundry pullovers, battledress, denims and leather jerkin: I looked like the Michelin tyre man! I hadn't seen much of Tom since we left Celles, as each troop had enough problems to overcome and there was little time for socialising.

Where were the Germans? The only ones we'd seen since crossing the Meuse were corpses, lying preserved in the deep snow. It was like chasing a will-o'-the-wisp: we'd hear we were going to put in an attack somewhere or other, but then it wouldn't materialise, so off we would go skating along the icy roads in another direction, only to find the intended action cancelled again.

Thursday 4 January was by far the worst day as far as the weather was concerned. Johnny Walker went forward to have a look at a couple of tanks in difficulty in front of us on the road, then came back and told our troop to go off the road to bypass the obstruction. We knew there was an almost perpendicular drop on either side of the road, but it looked all right, as there were a few trees here and there on the sloping surface before the edge, and the ground seemed firm enough.

Briton and *Brecon* preceded *Buzzard* as we gingerly went forward over the verge and across the snow-covered ground to the right of the highway. Joe drove *Buzzard* in the tracks made by the other two tanks, but their passage must have compacted the snow into hard ice because *Buzzard* suddenly slid crabwise onto the sloping ground leading to the edge of the precipice. We could hear Joe cursing like mad as he tried to get the tank under control, but to no avail. It gathered speed as it slid from side to side, knocking over a sapling, which was pulled out by its roots and crushed under the runaway tank. I froze as I recalled an incident during the drive from Maasbree to Nederweert, in which Captain Julius, our recce officer, was thrown clean out of the turret and decapitated as his tank went over on its side in a ditch.

I ducked instinctively into the turret, closed the hatch and prayed. Bob shouted to us over the IC to get out if we could, but before we had time to try the tank hit something with a thud and came to a stop. Joe immediately switched off the engine and we hardly dared move, in case even the slightest tremor caused the tank to slide again. Then Bob got slowly out of the turret and jumped down to size up the situation. I opened the hatch, poked my head out, and saw to my horror that the tank had come to a halt just a few yards from the edge of the steep drop to the valley below. *Buzzard*'s crew, with faces as white as the snow around us, gazed in wonder at the stump of a very large tree jammed under the rear of the tank and the offside track, which had saved us from almost certain disaster.

Johnny and our troop sergeant, Bradley, came to help. 'You were lucky that time, lads,' said Johnny, inspecting the stump. 'A few inches lower, and the tank would have gone clean over.' Joe peered down the valley, where the dotted farm buildings

123

looked like dolls' houses, then looked disconsolately at *Buzzard*. 'She just wouldn't respond to anything at all!'

'It would have been curtains for you lot, then,' said Sergeant Bradley, with a note of sympathy in his voice, and patted Joe on the back. I picked up a bit of the splintered stump and handed it to Owen as a memento of the day that *Buzzard* and her crew nearly finished up hurtling right over a precipice into oblivion.

Buzzard's rescue was accomplished after a lot of hard work and ingenuity on the part of the whole troop. A pathway was cleared through the snow, on which we threw stones and bracken to help the tracks over the icy ground. Then, with the assistance of steel towing cables from *Brecon* and *Briton*, *Buzzard* was slowly hauled from her precarious position. Joe was the sole occupant of the tank, and at first she refused to move as the other two tanks, engines labouring, struggled to free her. At the third attempt Buzzard shuddered a little and was pulled slowly away, to the rousing cheers of the crews watching. After unshackling the towing cables our troop continued the journey at the tail end of the squadron, eventually catching them up when they halted at the top of a hill before a long and steep descent ornamented with hairpin bends.

Johnny was summoned to a briefing with the CO and the other tank troop commanders, while we had a brew up. We stood drinking our hot tea on the equally hot engine hatch covers, warming our insides and our feet simultaneously. We soon learned, however, that standing on hot covers with soaking wet boots helps to warm the feet but ruins the boots in the process – the following day I trudged about in the snow with holes burnt through my leather soles, which were hanging on by a thread. An SOS for new boots for everyone was sent to the echelon; they were eventually issued with a warning about self-destruction of boots on hatch covers, and an order that this practice cease forthwith. Johnny returned from his pow-wow to announce that the squadron would finish the day's journey travelling across country. The recce officer had sorted out a route which cut out the perilous icy roads to our destination, the town of Barvaux. Our troop was the last to leave the road, by which time we could see the deep track marks of the leading troop descending the hill and ploughing through the virgin snow uphill about half a mile away. Joe was quite happy as he drove *Buzzard* down the slope. It was a relief for him to get off the road for a while.

Our journey took us over the snow-covered fields and through the rides of a snow-topped pine forest. As we emerged from the woods we were engulfed in a blizzard: I first noticed a rush of freezing, whistling wind, then a huge dark cloud rushing towards us, blotting out all light from the setting sun on the horizon. It stopped the whole squadron in its tracks, and we closed the hatches as the blizzard raged on for about half an hour. When we looked out we were astounded to see how much snow had drifted up at the front of the tank – almost to the height of the turret top. It was then all hands on deck clearing the snow, and we were wet, frozen through, and fed up by the time we were able to move on again. Ironically, the shelter of Barvaux was only a mile further on: if we'd been ten minutes earlier we would have been under cover somewhere when the blizzard struck. We had plenty more snow while we were in the Ardennes, but nothing could match the severity of that storm.

For another three days the ordeal of travelling on the terrible roads continued. Saturday 6 January was another terrible day: we were going through really mountainous terrain, and doing more walking than riding as we clambered in and out of the tanks helping others out of trouble. My diary records an occasion when I had to get out of the turret quickly: 'dropped hatch on two fingers. Smashed nails. Terrible pain.' It makes me wince even now as I remember it. Fortunately the hatch fell on the fingers of my left hand rather than my right, so it could have been worse, and the accident was only another trauma in a dreadful day of slogging through arctic conditions. That evening, like the previous night, the squadron harboured in a tiny hamlet – I didn't even record their names, as I was too miserable at the time to care.

After a restless night, with my fingers throbbing like mad, we continued our journey at first light. It was another nightmare on the terrible glassy roads, with intermittent snow showers to make things worse. Many tanks were ditched on the tortuous, steeply-winding, narrow roads of this very hilly region, and so much time was lost in helping out tanks in trouble that it was well after dark before the squadron arrived at its destination for the day, a place called Maffe. A count revealed that two of our 18 tanks hadn't arrived and I recorded this fact in my diary, along with the note 'Fingers aching intensely'.

We were frozen stiff, hungry and very fed up. Our blues disappeared, however, when Donk showed us to our quarters after parking our tanks in what appeared to be the private grounds of an estate. We trudged through the snow in the wake of the SSM, and in the darkness could just make out a very large building ahead of us: the Chateau Ramsay. After all we'd endured since crossing the Meuse ten days before, and the grotty places we had slept in, it was akin to entering paradise. Looking around at the opulent interior of this sumptuous chateau, we were overwhelmed by its splendour. It all seemed unreal. We couldn't believe our luck, and nor could we believe that this was to be our home for the next 12 days, standing by in case of a possible German counter-attack. We also dined in comparative luxury, with plenty of hot meals prepared for us in the chateau kitchen.

I now had time to mix with Tom, Punchy, the two Jocks and Bill Powland once again, and we managed to get a few trips out in the squadron jeep with Bill Hollowbread. We visited Jeneffe, Porcheresse and, on a couple of days, even went back to Dinant.

My diary for 11 January reads 'Got drunk with Bill and Joe on SM rum. Absolutely helpless.' We could have been court-martialled if we'd been caught by the orderly officer, as we were actually on guard duty at the time. We'd just been relieved and returned to the guard room to rest for our four hours off, and it started off innocently enough with Bill discovering SSM Donk Braybrook's hiding place for secreting the brown stone gallon bottle of issue rum. The three of us were frozen stiff, after being on patrol for two hours in below-freezing temperatures, and Bill poured a tot into each of our enamel mugs to warm us up.

'Donk won't miss that,' said Bill, as we drank the strong rum; but one tot led to another, and another. The rum was soon not only coursing through my stomach, setting it on fire, but also going to my head, sending me eventually into a deep sleep. The incoming guard found the three of us sprawled out on the floor of Donk's little office, with the uncorked bottle of rum in between us and luckily the right way up. We were roused and helped back to our own rooms to continue to sleep it off, but before we left Bill had just enough reasoning to replace the bottle in its hiding place. Nothing was heard from Donk afterwards, so I assume he didn't twig that someone had been at his rum.

Our comfortable stay at the Chateau Ramsay had to end some time, and the squadron left this desirable residence on 18 January. Although the weather had improved the road conditions were still very bad, but we were consoled by the shining sun and blue sky. These enabled our aircraft to make hay: from the hundreds of planes we saw, and the constant drone of aircraft engines, they were certainly giving the Germans a bashing.

We were moved about tactically for three days, either as a threat to the enemy or to prevent counter-attack. Our Ardennes adventures came to an end on 21 January, by which time Von Rundstedt's beaten armies were in full retreat eastward through the snowbound hills and wintry wooded terrain. Hitler's massive last-chance gamble of a winter offensive against the Allies had failed to reach the Meuse, let alone Brussels or Antwerp, and had thus failed to cut the Allied armies in two as planned.

Our tanks slithered down their last hill on our emergence from the Ardennes at the picturesque town of Namur on the River Meuse. There was a commanding view of flat terrain on the other side of the river, in great contrast to the mountainous region we had travelled through since crossing the Meuse at Dinant. The town looked lovely, and it was a pity that we weren't able to stay long enough to explore the place.

We crossed the bridge and met up with our old RASC friends at the top of the hill, where transporters were once again to take the regiment part of the way to our next destination. Loading *Buzzard* on the transporter, we were watched by some local people, and one kind elderly lady handed me a souvenir of Namur: ten small picture postcards of the town in a window envelope, two of which showed the bridge we had just crossed. It is a lasting memory of the completion of my Ardennes travels.

Chapter 13

The Battle of the Reichswald

The transporters took us to Diest, where the tanks were unloaded and we stayed the night in a lovely mansion. We continued our journey on our own tracks, travelling via Eindhoven to our destination at a village called Oirschot, about a dozen miles or so south of s'Hertogenbosch. Here, as in Tongres, the inhabitants opened up their houses to us and made us welcome and comfortable during our 11-day stay. So too did the brothers in a monastery college there, inviting us to an enjoyable party on 25 January. The monks entertained us with music and song and, as I noted in my diary, 'Tom and I do a turn'.

The following day we were invited to spend an afternoon with the brothers, taking part in indoor games and outdoor activities. There's always a first time for anything, and this was my initiation into ice skating on a frozen stream in the college grounds. The monks loaned us some rather crude wooden skates and I took to the ice: I found it very difficult to keep on my feet for a while, but gradually got the hang of things. It was great fun, even though we all had a few bruises by the end of the session - mainly from crashing into a low bridge that crossed the stream.

There was great excitement among the lads on 27 January, when the result of the ballot for UK leave was posted on the HQ board. The odds that Tom and I would be drawn to go on leave at the same time must have been about a million to one, and we didn't beat them. I drew number 377 and Tom drew 484, but I put my leave off to coincide with his dates, and a highly delighted holder of number 483 had his leave brought forward.

We also received post at Oirschot: I had a letter from Jean and Anna Baar-Bruls in Tongres, and another extremely loving one from Mini. I was really surprised by Mini's letter, suddenly seeing how infatuated she had become after knowing me for only a little over a week. She had obviously taken our short friendship far too seriously, not realising that to me she was just one of countless girls I had met in the course of my travels. I had no intention of getting serious with any of them!

With the same post came a letter from our sister Eileen, telling us that Tom's wife Rosie had given birth to a boy. It was quite plain to me that Tom considered his marriage completely dead, and he could find no compassion for her, saddled with a bastard as a result of her infidelity.

107 Regiment moved out of Oirschot after dusk on Saturday 3 February, amidst the tightest security imaginable. All tell-tale tactical signs on the tanks were obliterated, and rumour had it that at long last the Allies were to mount an offensive to drive the final nail into Hitler's coffin. Von Rundstedt's abortive Ardennes offensive had so weakened the German military capabilities that it was felt a massive attack would drive the enemy forces across the Rhine. Allied armies would then cross the river and advance into the very heart of Germany itself. Sounded all right, but we knew that, on Hitler's orders, the enemy would put up a fanatical resistance to any attack on German soil.

Our tanks travelled nose to tail throughout the night, moving painfully slowly along roads cluttered with traffic involved in the build-up for the offensive, which was only allowed to move during the hours of darkness. At first light we reached the road bridge over the River Waal at Nijmegen. It was an impressive sight, with a series of semi-circular iron spans stretching across the wide river. The regiment's tanks and transport were then concealed in a well-camouflaged harbour in the woods south of Nijmegen. It had taken the whole night to travel a distance of about 40 miles, and we were tired and hungry, so up went the bivouacs and out came the compo rations.

Next day, Monday 5 February, the regiment harboured in woods outside Heumen, a little town on the east side of the River

Maas about seven miles south of Nijmegen. It had been a miserable day, and was not improved when Lieutenant Walker briefed us on our role in the imminent attack. 107 Regiment was to support the 51st Highland Division on the right flank of the offensive, while the other two regiments of 34 Armoured Brigade, 147 RAC and 9th RTR, were to provide support for the 53rd Welsh Division on our left.

'We're going to attack and advance through the Siegfried Line and the Reichswald Forest,' said Johnny, making it sound as easy as a stroll down Petticoat Lane on a Sunday morning.

'Well, I've got the washing ready to hang out,' I said, at which point the troop broke into the chorus of the Siegfried Line song. Johnny waited with a smile on his face for the song to end before carrying on. The impending offensive was to be a massive five division attack on the enemy front, between the Rhine and the Maas. It was hoped and expected that the Germans would stand and fight to the last man to defend their own soil west of the Rhine, rather than withdraw across the river. Hitler could not conceivably agree to withdraw and give up a square inch of the Fatherland without a fight, so it would be a bloody battle of attrition.

Johnny was obviously looking forward to the coming fight, but the rest of the troop couldn't share his death-or-glory attitude to combat. We went into an attack resignedly, as a duty, whereas Johnny was never more excited than when the smell of battle was in his nostrils.

The regiment moved out of Heumen during the evening to an assembly area in woods closer to our point of attack. All movement by units involved in the coming operation was by night, and all units were under strict radio silence. By Wednesday 7 February everything was ready for the off, so Johnny took us to the edge of the woods to peep at the Siegfried Line and Reichswald Forest defences through binoculars. The low-lying terrain below us looked peaceful and harmless enough, but Johnny pointed out the anti-tank ditch in the far distance, and other obstacles and strongpoints relative to the 'defence overprints' recently issued. The Reichswald looked huge and sombre in the

131

background, with tall tree trunks seemingly so near to each other that it would be difficult to get a wheelbarrow through, let alone a Churchill tank. Johnny told us the enemy considered the forest to be an impenetrable natural tank obstacle, but we should aim to prove them wrong.

I must confess to a feeling of excitement and wonder as I looked through the binoculars and had my first glimpse of Germany. From schooldays it had been instilled in us as the land of the natural enemy, a view fuelled by constant media exposure of Hitler's Nazi domination and aggression since the early 1930s. Now, after nearly six years of struggle and sacrifice, the sword, in the shape of the mighty military power of the Allies, was poised to strike into the heart of Germany. They were about to get a taste of their own medicine.

We were to move from the start line at 10.30am, Johnny told us, although we couldn't expect any sleep after the artillery barrage started in the early hours. The attack had been masterminded by General Horrocks, the tall, gaunt commander of 30 Corps, whom we had seen recently on a tour of the forward areas with some other high-rankers, including our own Brigadier W. S. Clarke.

Trudging back to our harbour through the woods we were ankle-deep in wet earth: a thaw had set in since we left Oirschot, which combined with a few days of rain to turn the surface into a sea of mud. Sergeant Bradley remarked to Lieutenant Walker that the conditions could be worse for the tanks than at Blerick. 'Infinitely worse,' replied Johnny cheerfully, knocking dollops of mud off his boots with a stick before disappearing into his bivouac and emerging again immediately with a bottle in his hand. He poured schnapps into each trooper's mug, and proposed a toast to the safe and successful conclusion of the Reichswald battle. We all downed the spirits in one gulp.

I spent a couple of hours that evening with Tom and Punchy in their troop space, and we were joined by Bill Powland, Jock Gould and Tommy Reilly. Tommy strummed his guitar while we sang a few songs, but after the strains of 'Kiss Me

Goodnight, Sergeant-Major' had died away we decided the prospect of Donk doing just that was too awful to contemplate, and ended our sing-song before he could put in an appearance.

It was all very peaceful and quiet as I made my way back to my own troop. It was difficult to imagine that within twelve hours our tanks would be advancing from this wood to fight the Germans on their own soil.

During the night I took my turn on guard: it was raining and very cold. At times like this your mind concentrates only on the anxieties within, and pushes them to the forefront. All sorts of things are conjured up and sent racing through the brain, to be magnified out of all proportion to their realities. Uppermost in my thoughts was a sense of foreboding about the coming conflict: once again the Dyson twins were going into battle in their respective tanks, only a stone's throw apart. We'd been very lucky to have survived so far, considering the high rate of casualties inflicted on our squadron since landing in Normandy. With each battle, however, the odds against us both coming through unscathed were dwindling. I was glad when it was time to wake up Joe Whelan to take over from me on guard duty.

Once inside my blankets, I went off into a deep sleep almost as soon as my head touched my makeshift pillow, and the next thing I can recall was being abruptly woken, sitting up startled at the deafening noise of guns. It was the start of our softening-up barrage, and so incredibly intense that we had to shout at one another to be heard. We learned later that it was the heaviest barrage employed by the British Army during the entire war in Europe, and it almost shook us out of our beds.

The whole squadron soon congregated outside to watch the spectacle, with the ground shaking beneath our feet. Tracer shells from Bofors guns whizzed over us in their thousands. Multiple rockets from our 'mattress' batteries swished across ceaselessly, and the constant fire from hundreds of machine guns added variety to the cacophony of ear-splitting noise assailing the morning air. I pulled the waterproof hood of my tank suit over my balaclava, to muffle my ears as well as protect myself from the fine drizzle of rain.

The replacement members of our troop, who had yet to take part in a battle, were visibly shaken by the intensity of the barrage, and also by Johnny's shouted warning that the Germans would fight hard when we attacked them despite the artillery bombardment. They, like thousands of other reinforcements brought in to replace high numbers of British casualties, were about to be 'blooded'. The battle-hardened veterans among us did our best to allay their fears, but we knew from our own experience that inwardly they were very scared young men, shipped out here after just a short training period in Britain.

The bombardment went on with only intermittent breaks for over five hours, while we busied ourselves preparing for the attack: eating, washing and shaving as the light dawned on a cold, grey morning. In battle or not, I never missed out on a morning shave, unlike some in the squadron, who went for days while we were in action before condescending to have a scrape. A small minority left something to be desired when it came to personal hygiene: some had been known to go in and out of the mobile bath tent without a drop of water touching their bodies. We brewed up our fifth cuppa since the start of the barrage, and dragged at cigarettes to steady our nerves.

Radio silence was lifted when Johnny returned from a briefing and ordered operators to net in on the frequency. Hundreds of RAF bombers had passed over us the night before and Johnny told us they had successfully flattened Cleve and Goch in the attack. This gave us a fillip, as we reasoned it would delay any reinforcements to the enemy defenders in the Reichswald.

We were now all ready, waiting tensely in our tanks at the edge of the wood. The creeping barrage looked as if it had pulverised everything in its path as far as we could see. Shells were still raining down, with the Reichswald Forest in the distance acting as a background to explosions, fires and overhanging smoke everywhere. We could also see the deep track marks of the Funnies that had followed up behind the artillery barrage to flail through the minefields and bridge the formidable anti-tank ditch with fascines. We heard over the radio that many of Hobart's Funnies were in difficulties, as their tracks turned the soft, thawing ground into a mass of clinging mud. It was a foretaste of what lay in store for us.

Precisely at 10.30am came the order from Lieutenant Walker for the troop to advance. Joe Whelan started the engine up and away we went, through the trees and out into the open country, ready to fight our way through the Siegfried Line and the Reichswald Forest.

As we advanced, with the infantry of the 51st Highland Division hurrying forward purposefully, we were greeted by a truly unforgettable sight. On all sides, as far as the eye could see, were jerkin-clad men wearing tin helmets and carrying equipment on their backs, with trenching spades on top of their haversacks. Most of them had rifles at the ready and some were carrying Bren guns. In their midst the Churchill supporting tanks rolled forward, with exhausts emitting smoke into the cold air and their tracks cutting deep grooves in the soft, green turf.

Now we were on the move my butterflies disappeared, and the tenseness inside me gradually relaxed and gave way to a sense of exhilaration and excitement, mixed with a little trepidation. Our troop advanced slowly behind the Jocks of the Black Watch, who were warily probing their way forward in the direction of some ruined buildings about halfway between the start line and the anti-tank ditch. We wove our way in and out between the shell craters as if in a slalom. Smoke lingered all over the area, and the air reeked with the smell of spent explosives.

Looking through my periscope I could see no signs of the enemy in or near the first objective, but the Jocks were taking no chances. They advanced in leapfrog fashion from one shell hole to the next, taking turns to give covering fire with rifles and Bren guns, until they came within striking distance of the buildings. Then there was a lull in activity while the Black Watch officer approached our troop, seemingly indifferent to any danger, and held his hand up to signal us to halt. He climbed aboard Johnny's tank for a short discussion before jumping down and returning to his forward troops.

The infantry company commander wanted us to hold our fire while he sent a raiding party into the buildings, so our tanks stood to and waited on further orders. The Jocks of the Black Watch rushed forward, bayonets fixed, with shouts and screams that could be heard above the other sounds of battle, and disappeared into the buildings. They emerged with little groups of German prisoners with hands on their heads: they had apparently been there all the time, crouching in the cellars in a state of shock. The barrage had done most to reduce them to this condition, but the final straw must have been glimpsing the blood-curdling charge of the Jocks, with the cold steel glinting at the end of their rifles. It looked terrifying enough even viewed from the rear.

The first objective had been taken with no casualties, which was a relief, but we were still on Dutch territory. The ease of this attack probably led to a little over-confidence in the next, and resulted in the infantry suffering quite a few casualties.

Our troop drove into the group of buildings while the RAMC lads were stretchering away some wounded Germans. I opened the hatch and took a look at the shambles all around. Some enemy corpses had been mangled by shells in the bombardment, and were a gruesome sight – too sickening for one young Jock, who looked to be still in his teens. He was bent over spewing up as his companion, an unshaven, grizzled veteran, tried to comfort him. Looking up at me, he grimaced and remarked angrily, 'Och, 'tis bairns they be sinding doon ta us fer feeting, noo.' I could only agree that they seemed to be scraping the barrel for reinforcements.

We took a breather here, waiting for the whole squadron to assemble before going on towards the Reichswald Forest. Tom's troop was the last to arrive, and I ran over to have a few words with him. They'd been delayed pulling their troop commander's tank out of some deep mud. We stood together and urinated down the side of his tank. It was supposed to bring luck.

Shortly afterwards we continued the advance, amidst signs that the Germans were getting over the terror and shock of the shelling and starting to fight back. Sporadic small arms fire sent up spurts of earth among the infantry as they dashed forward, spreadeagling themselves under cover to fire at their targets. Our tanks took turns to help the infantry capture various pill-boxes, houses and barns leading up to the anti-tank ditch. The enemy were sending over 'stonks' of mortar shells, scattering the infantry as they dived into shell craters to shelter from flying fragments of shrapnel.

The Black Watch were suffering casualties now, and wounded infantry were mixed with the German prisoners taken back past us, with the more seriously injured stretchered back by medics. Dead men lay where they fell. The going was getting worse for our tanks, and it took time to tow out those which became bogged down in the oozing mud. *Buzzard* was one of the victims, with Joe cursing like mad as he realised we were sinking into the bog. We came to an abrupt halt, with the tracks racing away and sending up piles of mud, until Joe gave it up as a bad job and stopped the engine.

Sergeant Bradley radioed over the B-set that he would come to our aid, and within minutes had manoeuvred his tank to *Buzzard*'s front. Owen and I fastened the towing cable to the tank, feeling rather naked outside *Buzzard*'s armoured protection. Fearing a sniper's bullet we hurried about our task, wallowing in the mud up to our knees. A hand signal told the sergeant to begin the tow, his tank inched forward on firmer ground, and slowly but surely *Buzzard* was pulled out of the marsh. We unhitched the wire rope from the tank in front and replaced it on *Buzzard*'s exterior with alacrity, then hurriedly returned to relative safety inside the tank.

The troop rejoined the squadron just a stone's throw from the anti-tank ditch, which stretched across the battlefield for miles. The infantry had gone to ground when we arrived on the scene, and we soon realised why: sporadic bursts of Spandau fire and the single cracks of snipers' guns were coming from a group of buildings near the anti-tank obstacle. The rapid fire of the Spandaus suggested there were three or four guns operating in the shelter of the buildings. The enemy strongpoint clearly had to be eliminated.

Once again I saw the Black Watch company commander unhurriedly approach our leading tank for a short discussion. His apparently nonchalant behaviour, amid enemy sniper fire spattering up little eruptions of dirt all over the area as bullets landed, was unbelievable! He intended to make an all-out assault to force a crossing over the anti-tank ditch, and needed to plan the tank support with our squadron leader. The outcome of their meeting was that our troop was detailed to provide close support for the infantry. We grumbled resignedly over our bad luck.

Our troop advanced at the appointed time, and systematically fired HE shells from hull-down positions at the supposed lairs of Spandau teams. As our shots hit and exploded, sending fragments of debris flying into the air, we really thought we had put paid to the machine gun nests. The infantry assumed so too, as only sniper fire was now coming from the enemy, and moved forward in little spurts towards the anti-tank ditch under cover of a smoke-screen from our shells. All seemed to be going well until the assault was halted in its tracks by bursts of Spandau fire. We could see to our horror that these claimed some victims, and the infantry were forced to withdraw hurriedly to avoid further casualties. Johnny Walker then informed us over the B-set that he was going forward on foot 'to see what the form was'.

He returned to tell us that the Black Watch company commander was among those killed. We were appalled at the news: only a short while ago we'd seen him liaising with our commander. It might be said that his air of nonchalance under sniper fire was rather foolhardy; I prefer to believe that it was his way of inspiring his men and giving them confidence in his leadership. They had certainly shown it in the brave dash across the bridge, which ended so tragically when their commander was mown down by enemy machine gun fire.

The infantry had also lost some of their platoon commanders, and had become disorganised, so Johnny decided to direct them personally in mounting another attack. We watched, spellbound, as he went about the task. He moved between the infantry and us, directing our HE fire at designated targets. When he was convinced we had succeeded in putting the Spandaus out of action, we lobbed over a few more smoke shells and the infantry attempted another crossing. *Buzzard*'s crew cheered in unison as the Jocks charged forward, this time amidst only desultory small arms fire, and succeeded in reaching the other side of the anti-tank obstacle in numbers and disappearing into the landscape. Our troop then followed them over to consolidate the position.

The enemy was now concealed in a group of buildings on the far side of the ditch, but this next attack was rather an anti-climax after what had gone before. In a vengeful mood after passing fallen comrades in the stiff positions induced by rigor mortis, and supported by fire from our tanks, the Jocks infiltrated the buildings with bayonets fixed, and the enemy capitulated without firing a shot.

It was rather surprising that only a handful of German defenders were led back into captivity. Were some of the Jocks overstepping the mark in their desire for retribution? One would never know, but when we drove up and dismounted among the group of buildings we had a look around. The enemy had certainly paid dearly for the staunch fight they put up to prevent us crossing the anti-tank ditch, as proven by the number of corpses. It seemed to be a disproportionately high rate of casualties, though, compared to what we usually expected.

Johnny Walker was in an exultant mood as the troop gathered around our three tanks for a pow-wow before moving off again. 'Well done, lads. We're the first troop in the regiment to cross the anti-tank ditch, the outer perimeter of the Siegfried Line defences. It should make you all feel very proud of yourselves.' Sergeant Bradley, laconic as ever, removed his pipe from his mouth and said, 'As a reward they'll probably send us into the Reichswald first, too.' We sniggered at the evident sarcasm in his remark, but Johnny took it as a compliment.

Meanwhile A Squadron, who were supporting a company of Black Watch on our left, were having even more difficulty than us with the conditions. Their flail tanks clearing a pathway through the minefield were getting bogged down, slowing up the advance on that sector, as we heard over the A-set. C Squadron was following up in the wake of A and B in the order of advance.

It wasn't long before the rest of B Squadron crossed over the bridged tank obstacle and joined us in the shelter of a copse. Looking back we could see a long queue of vehicles waiting their turn to get across: flail tanks, Crocodile flamethrowing tanks, bridging tanks, infantry carriers and supply trucks, all starting to pour through the breach in the defence created by the Jocks with the support of our troop. Surveying the scene, I felt a sense of pride at taking part in the assault which had made it possible. The final accolade came from Tom, who sought me out as soon as his troop joined us. Creeping up behind me, he hung his beret on the binoculars through which I was looking, suddenly blotting out the vision, then slapped me on the back and enthused about my troop's action. His congratulations were cut short, however, as we came under mortar fire which sent us scurrying back inside our tanks.

We waited until A Squadron had crossed the anti-tank ditch before advancing any further: our objective was to help the infantry infiltrate and establish themselves on the fringe of the Reichswald before darkness descended. The forest looked very much larger and more forbidding now we were on the halfway mark. It was a daunting prospect, but when A Squadron and their infantry on our left were ready to advance we moved forward with the infantry in little groups.

There was an immediate response from the enemy, concealed on the edge of the forest. Our infantry dashed forward from one bit of cover to another, under constant fire from Spandaus and snipers, but pressed on bravely and relentlessly. The tanks, rolling forward between stages of the advance, peppered the front of the forest with Besa fire. The going was heavy and some tanks got bogged down in the mud, so Johnny said it was by the luck of the draw that our troop happened to be in the lead when the CO of a company of Gordon Highlanders requested tank support for the assault on the enemy in the forest fringe. We preferred to believe that Johnny's daring leadership and tactically successful relationship with the infantry in the assault on the anti-tank obstacle had inspired the squadron leader to order our troop forward in close support once again.

We were now only about two hundred yards or so from the forest, and the devastating effect the barrage had wreaked on the trees could be clearly seen through binoculars. Huge trunks of tall pines had been snapped and broken by the pounding, and were

140

lying on the ground or hanging down still attached by shreds. Shattered branches littered the forest floor. Here and there grey-clad corpses of German defenders stood out against the darkness of the debris beneath the trees; some bodies still whole, some in bits after being blown to smithereens by the tremendous bombardment that morning. The close-up view was grim, but the fast rat-tat of Spandau teams and sounds of rifle fire coming from the woods showed there were still a lot of enemy dug in.

We were in the last wooded area before the forest, with only a bit of open, shell-pocked ground separating us from the enemy. Our troop commander scurried about the area with the infantry commander, sizing up the situation through binoculars from prone positions. Then Johnny scampered back towards us, happy as a boy scout at a jamboree as he issued the troop plan of attack over the B-set. 'Guns to the right of them, guns to the left of them, volleyed and thundered. Into the valley of death rode the six hundred,' chanted Taffy mockingly. Bob Bolton countered him with a laugh. 'That was the Charge of the Light Brigade. We're the heavy mob, and we've got the guns right here,' patting the breech block of the 75mm turret gun with his right hand as he spoke. The banter helped to alleviate the tension building up inside us.

Our tanks moved forward with the infantry, our Besas raking fire along the fringe of the woods, until we were about a hundred yards away. Then, with blood-curdling shouts, the Jocks charged the rest of the way over the open ground with rifles and bayonets fixed, braving some defensive fire in the process. A few were mown down, their bodies writhing in pain, or just collapsing and lying inert in the positions in which they hit the ground. The vast majority, however, continued into the trees, where we could see them dashing about in little groups attacking Germans in the trenches there. It was an eyeball-to-eyeball skirmish, and lasted for about an hour before the enemy succumbed and gave the Gordons a toehold on German soil.

We were called upon to pour Besa and HE shell fire at more troublesome fortified defences inside the forest, and Johnny was

141

kept busy directing our fire as we drove into suitable positions among the trees. Our main fear as we entered the gloomy, dripping, dark woods, crushing fallen timber under our tracks and knocking down saplings in our way, was the Panzerfaust. Although designed to be thrown away after use, the German hand-held anti-tank weapon was quite capable of penetrating and brewing up a Churchill at close quarters. We kept a close watch as we went in and out of the trees, but the only Germans I saw were incapable of firing – they were already dead. Joe did his best to get round the corpses that lay in our path, but some were mangled further under our tracks. It was unavoidable under the circumstances, but bits of bone, flesh and blood became mixed with the mud of the forest and embedded in our tracks.

Johnny Walker was more often out of his tank than in it, liaising with the infantry and guiding our tanks on foot to bring our fire to bear. 'He's got more lives than our cat,' commented Bob Bolton, as Johnny scurried about the woods with the infantry commanders. They achieved their objective of getting the infantry firmly established just before dark, and our troop emerged from the forest, our task completed. It had been a hard-won victory, though, in which the Germans had fought to the death as predicted, and gave us a warning of what to expect when we continued our advance. But for now it was a matter of consolidating the area, and we could see by the many troop carriers around that a sizeable force of infantry was established in well dug-in positions inside the forest.

Our troop stood by out in the open, observing jeeps, Bren gun carriers and transport arrive as the Gordons set up their HQ at the edge of the forest. Some of the vehicles had to be towed to free them from clogging mud, made worse now by the amount of traffic. *Buzzard*'s crew dismounted for a breath of fresh air, and Joe took the opportunity to tighten up a loose track caused by heavy going over the debris in the forest. That was the point at which we noticed the grisly remains of human bodies, in little pieces, around the tracks and bogey wheels.

'Ugh!' shouted Joe, as he stopped tightening the track with a huge spanner and took a closer look at something that had fallen down by his feet. The object of his disdain was part of a hand, complete with fingers. We stood gaping at it for a few seconds in morbid curiosity. Bob still had a spade in his hands, having just returned from a lavatory stop, and acted quickly. Digging another hole just to the side of *Buzzard*, he shovelled the hand in and replaced the earth. 'At least that part of him has had a decent burial,' he remarked.

Late that evening we rejoined the rest of our squadron, harboured in the copse from which we had launched our attack that afternoon. Tom came round as soon as he knew our troop had arrived, and we chatted before I rejoined my crew to prepare something to eat from our compo rations. The troop congregated around our tanks to discuss the recent action, and some anecdotes were bizarre. Sergeant Bradley described how, going through the forest, he spied a German halfway up a tree on a large bough. Ducking down inside the turret, he drew his revolver ready to fire, then peered over the edge to take aim. The German was motionless, so he ordered his tank forward, but as it passed the tree, giving the trunk a glancing blow, the German was dislodged from his perch. The falling body just missed the sergeant as it bounced off the turret and landed on the ground, with a rifle still clutched in lifeless hands. 'Rock-a-bye Jerry, in the tree-top,' chimed one of his crew.

The incident with the hand was on my mind as I tried to get to sleep in the tank that night. Was it a sign of the hand of doom? Some omen of impending danger? I was immune to seeing all the gore of mutilated bodies, so why should a little thing like that prey on my mind? It had a subconscious effect: in the middle of the night I dreamt I could see a hand, dripping with blood, coming down through the hatch and about to close round my neck. 'No! No!' I shouted. Then I woke up with a start: I could feel drips on my face, and I touched my wet skin nervously and looked at my fingers, fearing it was blood. It wasn't. The rain was coming down in torrents, judging by the sound of it lashing down on the turret, and there was a leak just above my head. It was reassuring to see Bob and Taffy in the dim light of the turret, snoring away in contentment. I changed my position, and vowed to do something about that leak the next day, before dropping off into a deep and untroubled sleep.

It was just getting light as I peered through the periscope, and the rain was still pelting down. I kept the bad dream a secret, fearing ridicule from the lads, but the memory reawakened my sense of foreboding. The squadron moved out that morning alongside the infantry to deal with a number of enemy fortified positions on the southern fringes of the forest, which had to be eliminated before we could mount an assault on the Siegfried Line defences from the Reichswald to the River Maas.

Individual troops and infantry engaged in a series of actions under the most atrocious conditions. The continuous heavy rain had turned the ground into deep, sticky mud - paradise for a hippopotamus, but not so for tanks, let alone the poor old infantry footsloggers, up to their knees in it. Mines were an additional hazard, and in mined areas under direct Spandau fire from the enemy there were casualties among crews engaged in repairs to damaged tracks. On one occasion our troop was ordered forward to assist another troop under fire, with two of their tanks hit by mines and the crews busy repairing the tracks. As *Buzzard* passed one of the disabled tanks, I saw Sergeant 'Dusty' Miller and the rest of his white-faced and shaken crew taking shelter nearby. I knew how they must feel after *Buzzard*'s encounter with the mine in Normandy.

Johnny Walker liaised with the infantry commander to organise an attack on the enemy position. The Spandau nest was pinpointed and our troop advanced, firing HE shells at the target as we went and following up with a hail of fire from our Besas. The Jocks then rushed into the forest and went about their business purposefully and efficiently, returning in little groups with sullen-looking prisoners shuffling along with hands on their heads.

The Germans, now alerted to the fact that they were facing a full-scale offensive on this front, were rushing in reserves to counter our attacks. Fighting was stiffer, and the first signs of SP anti-tank guns were reported by the infantry. Our tanks were forced to penetrate deeper into the forest to assist the infantry as they battled their way forward, fighting for every yard against a fanatical enemy.

As news came over the A-set of the first of our tanks being knocked out by an 88 AP shell from an SP gun, decapitating the front gunner, it became a cat-and-mouse affair. We were edgy all the time. In parts of the forest the trees were so close and their trunks so thick that even our Churchills couldn't crash their way through, and it was usually when we skirted around these areas and took to the rides that we came under fire from well-concealed SP guns. We also found mines scattered around in the vicinity, including the dreaded anti-personnel or 'foot' mines. These diabolical weapons were predominantly triggered off by the infantry, but some of our crews were unlucky at times.

Young Alan, in Sergeant Bradley's tank, had joined the troop only the previous day to replace an injured crew member. We came upon a dense, impassable area in the forest, and Johnny Walker ordered the troop sergeant and troop corporal to follow his tank driving along a track for a while until we could get back into the woods. Our tank followed behind the sergeant's tank for about fifty yards, then there was a huge explosion and we saw the tank lurch over slightly. The crew baled out and ran for cover; then we heard a smaller explosion and saw, to our horror, one of them drop to the ground amid a small pall of smoke and falling debris. It was Alan.

Bob heaved himself out of the turret and ran to see what he could do to help the lad, writhing about a few yards away from the track, and was joined by Bradley and Johnny. I could see the explosion had ripped away the lower part of the boy's trousers and tank suit. The left leg was exposed and looked like shredded raw meat, with bits of what used to be a wool sock clinging to it. The lad was treated on the spot with shell dressings from the tank first aid box, and a message was sent over the radio for a medic.

While waiting for medical assistance for Alan, the sergeant's crew busied themselves repairing the broken track. The enemy made the most of the situation, though, and they came under heavy sniper fire. Bob rushed back and ordered me to lob over some smoke bombs through the turret ejector; the other two tanks did the same, and soon we had laid a thick smoke-screen in front of the troop, providing an effective shield against enemy snipers. We could still hear shots, but they were firing blind. The doctor arrived very soon, and accompanied the injured man back by stretcher in a half-track vehicle. We heard the good news later: the explosion had merely torn away part of the flesh below the knee, and young Alan would in time regain full use of his leg. His fleetness of foot haring away from the tank probably saved him from a worse injury.

With the sergeant's tank repaired but minus one crew member, our troop carried on the advance. The infantry combed the woods on either side of the track in the pouring rain – and it continued to pour down, in fact, with only short breaks, for about twenty days. We were making very slow progress because of the conditions, and the poor infantry suffered casualties from the pencil or foot mines strewn about the area.

As we rounded a slight bend in the track we came under fire from an anti-tank gun, so we immediately threw out smoke. The gun carried on sending AP shells whistling through the air, but failed to register a direct hit on our tanks. Johnny dismounted and ordered the troop to withdraw out of the line of fire, then went into a huddle with an infantry platoon officer. When infantry scouts returned with details of the SP gun location, about two hundred yards beyond the bend on the right-hand side, Johnny put his plan into action.

Under cover of a smoke-screen, the troop leader's tank and *Buzzard* turned the bend and fired round after around of HE shells and a hail of Besa fire in the direction of the gun position. I was too busy loading and reloading HE shells for Taffy to fire, and lobbing smoke bombs through the turret bomb thrower, to worry about anything. After going about a hundred yards along the track our tanks were able to get back inside the forest, and the infantry went forward: they were delighted to find the SP gun had been destroyed and its crew killed. Our well-aimed attack also put the rest of the enemy in the area to flight, and enabled the advance through the forest in our sector to continue.

We were all by now feeling the strain of fighting at close range.

146

The enemy had good reason to consider the forest an effective anti-tank obstacle, and strong resistance put up by crack German reinforcements in well-prepared defensive positions was taking its toll, both in casualties among the crews and knocked-out or damaged tanks. Battling our way through the dense, gloomy and muddy forest was claustrophobic. It seemed as if we were fighting our own little war, with only radio communication on the A-set between our troops and squadron HQ as evidence of similar actions taking place all the way through the forest.

Our troop was stood down at the end of the day by the infantry commander, after our advance had been halted by the fall of darkness. He had a chat with our troop commander and paid us a compliment as he left, calling out congratulations and thanks to the crews standing around our tanks. It was nicer still of him, as we learned from Johnny Walker, to offer to post infantry guards around our troop that night and give us some unbroken sleep. The fact that the rain was still dripping down from the tall pine trees made the concession even more welcome!

Supplies of petrol and ammunition arrived in a half-track that night, but, to the consternation of our rumbling tummies, no compo rations. We were forced to rummage over what was left from yesterday's ration box, pooled and shared between the troop, which amounted to a measured drop of self-heating soup and a couple of hard biscuits each. Scant fare after a day fighting our way through the Reichswald extension of the Siegfried Line. It was just as well there was enough compo tea to make a brew, otherwise Johnny would have had a mutiny on his hands. Bill Hollowbread, the half-track driver, had only a shrug of his shoulders when we questioned him about our rations. He'd hung on as long as he could before leaving: the ration truck must have broken down, or got bogged, or something...

It would be late the following morning before we received our next compo rations, and in the meantime we had plenty of boiled sweets to suck. It was a case of grin and bear it - or, in this instance, grumble and bear it. We rigged up a shelter from the rain by stretching our bivouac sheets between the tanks, and shared the frugal repast. Endeavouring to pour oil on troubled waters,

Johnny Walker made sure the wet and miserable crews had a rum ration, which went a long way to appeasing the troop and putting fire in our bellies - pouring rum on troubled waters!

Bill Hollowbread brought a message from Tom to say he'd come through the day's actions safely, and this knowledge combined with the rum to give me a good sleep. I was woken by loud banging noises on the tank echoing through the turret: the Jocks using the butts of their rifles to give us an early call at first light. It was another cold, grey morning, and it was still raining. We brewed up the last of the compo tea, but there was nothing to eat and we were famished. We sat bickering and chatting as we dreamed up new ways of cooking army boots, but the roar of an engine stopped the conversation immediately. We prepared ourselves for instant action, then relaxed when we recognised the recce officer in an armoured car stopping at Johnny Walker's tank.

Chapter 14

Up Against the Siegfried Line

Like the curate's egg, our next assignment was only good in parts. Good, because we were being withdrawn from the abominable fighting conditions in the Reichswald Forest. Bad, because we were being sent to more open country south of the Reichswald to take part in an assault against the much-vaunted concrete fortifications of the Siegfried Line. But if 107 Regiment had a tough assignment, it was equally if not more tough for the rest of our 34th Tank Brigade: 147 Regiment RAC and 9th RTR were having a very hard time supporting the 53rd Welsh Division fighting their way through the centre of the forest. They were making steady progress, however, in spite of the adverse conditions and stiff enemy resistance. This enabled us to be switched south now we had assisted the infantry in destroying the enemy strongpoints along the southern edge of the forest.

Our troop emerged from the gloom of the trees into the open early that morning, to join the squadron convoy forming up for the drive to the low-lying country south of the Reichswald. We crossed over the border back into Holland again on our way to the assembly area, driving through a deserted frontier post with a striped pole in pieces on the verge of the road.

The squadron strength had been reduced by casualties since the attack started two days before, and none of those who fought in the Reichswald could ever forget the deep, cloying mud. I am reminded of it every time I hear the song 'Mud, Mud, Glorious Mud'. The glory belonged to those of our gallant comrades who fought and died, or were injured, in the quagmire there.

The main objective for the 51st Highland Division was now the town of Goch, two or three miles inside the massive Siegfried Line fortifications. But Goch was still quite a distance away, and there were a lot of Germans in good fortified positions to be overcome before we reached the Siegfried Line. We thought the experience our regiment had acquired in the assault against the concrete fortifications, minefields and anti-tank ditches at Le Havre would stand us in good stead when the time came, and this would also be true for both the Funnies of the 79th Armoured Division and the 51st Highland Infantry lads.

Our first attack, later that day, was in support of the Seaforths. Their target was to assault and cross a bridge over a tributary of the River Maas at Buizengicht, which had to be taken and secured before we could launch a full-scale attack to capture the fortified town of Gennep and protect the right flank of the advance. There were a few pockets of enemy to be eliminated from houses, farm buildings and dug-in positions on this side of the bridge, and it was more our line of work than fighting in the confines of a pine forest. We felt a little happier, anyway, as we advanced to engage the enemy and support the Jocks.

In a series of leapfrogging actions the squadron troops made slow but steady progress towards the river crossing, but by the evening the enemy were still holding up our attempts to capture the bridge. They occupied the few remaining houses alongside the road leading down to the river, and were giving the infantry a lot of trouble as darkness fell.

The Jocks settled themselves into position for the night, and the squadron harboured in a group of farm buildings that had been occupied by the enemy only hours before. Our troop made ourselves reasonably comfortable in the pigsty. The pigs had gone, although the stench remained, but it was still preferable to spending another night inside our tanks. We didn't go hungry that night: earlier in the day we'd received two days' supply of compo boxes to make up for our missing rations. Johnny Walker had made sure about that, and also ensured we received an issue of rum later in the evening.

While we were standing around in the cold and draughty pigsty, drinking our rum, smoking, and chatting away, we noticed a difference in our usually cheerful troop leader. He was rather quiet and withdrawn, not joining in the conversation. By the dim light we'd rigged up on a lead from the tank battery we could see that his face was pale and drawn, and he didn't look too well. Joe Whelan asked him if he felt all right, but Johnny insisted that all he needed was a tot of rum to set him up. We carried on talking, but we could sense there was something troubling him. I tried to draw him into a discussion about the Russian offensive, advancing from the River Vistula to the River Oder, and presumably destined to end up looting and raping in Berlin. Johnny would normally have an opinion on the strategic implications of military matters, but said not a word. Shortly afterwards he left us to see one of the other troop officers, and we speculated as to what was on his mind.

'He's probably the most active troop leader in the squadron, and he's been taking a lot of risks these last few days,' said Sergeant Bradley. The conversation changed, and we were still jawing away when Johnny returned. He looked a little better, but remained quiet for the rest of the evening. The following morning Johnny seemed more like his normal self, so we assumed he must have been physically and mentally exhausted the previous night, and that a good sleep had recharged his batteries. He was full of beans as he returned from a briefing with the CO to instruct us for the day: we must go all out to capture the bridge and put in an attack against Gennep before evening.

'That's more like our Johnny,' I said, as *Buzzard*'s crew mounted the tank and got ready to move off at a moment's notice.

'Yeh, the smell of a battle ahead has revived him,' replied Joe. 'I just hope this won't be another River Orne.'

The circumstances were indeed very similar, and we wondered if we would get across the bridge here only to be counter-attacked and decimated as at the Orne bridgehead. The morning was cloudy, but the rain had stopped when our troop moved off with a group of infantry aboard our tanks. All the squadron troops ferried Jocks to the start line, where they descended and we waited for the order to advance. They seemed a cheerful lot, but

151

sometimes the broad Scots dialect was hard to understand. I commented to Bob that Tommy Reilly and Jock Gould would have no trouble with their lingo!

After a number of individual attacks by our tanks and infantry a determined enemy finally succumbed, but it was mid-morning before we forced them to retreat to the far side of the river. They made a stand in some houses on the other side of the bridge. Our troop advanced on the right-hand side of the approach road and came to a halt at the top of a slope leading down to the river. There were a few trees in front of us, but we could see the bridge and a large house on the far bank through gaps in the trees. We could hear Spandau and sniper fire as Johnny jumped down from his tank and dashed through the trees to have a word with the infantry commander, crouching down beside the officer's spreadeagled form to observe enemy positions on the far bank through binoculars.

Meanwhile the other tank troops and infantry had concentrated around the road leading down to the bridge, and the enemy judged it time to send over their 'moaning minnies'. Mortar shells landed all around us, so Bob and I dodged quickly down into the turret and closed our hatch cover pretty sharpish. Looking through my periscope I could see the explosions and flying debris as the shells hit the ground. One of the missiles landed just a few yards from *Buzzard* with a deafening blast, and a shower of shrapnel and earth descended on our tank, sounding for a few seconds like a roll on a kettledrum.

We had four inches of steel protecting us, but the men outside were not so fortunate. As soon as the shelling died down we saw a jeep with a red cross flag on a pole drive up, to attend to wounded infantry before taking them away. Johnny Walker returned to his tank during the lull, and contacted the squadron CO on the A-set to outline his plan.

We moved about a hundred yards to the right, and fired HE shells at the targets Johnny had selected while observing the enemy with the infantry commander. Taffy was in his element, firing shells as fast as I could load them into the breech. Other tank troops joined in the bombardment from their positions, and soon

152

smoke and flames could be seen coming from buildings on the other side of the river. Some grey-clad figures ran away from the large house nearest the bridge; a few fell under the hail of fire from infantry Brens and tank Besas, but the rest scurried to cover.

One of our troops was ordered forward to support the infantry in an assault crossing of the bridge, while other troops fired smoke shells to give an effective screen on the other side of the river and aimed Besa guns blindly through the smoke at the enemy positions. We kept our fingers crossed as the infantry rushed across the bridge, followed by one troop of tanks: I noticed Jock Gould and Tommy Reilly among the crews, as I read the names on the sides of the tanks advancing down the approach road. The little force established a bridgehead on the other side, and by midday the whole squadron had enlarged the bridgehead while the infantry consolidated the area. The battle for the bridge at Buizengicht had been won, after very fierce resistance by the enemy and with many casualties on both sides. The bridgehead was secure.

The squadron halted to enable crews to replenish stocks of ammunition and top-up with petrol if necessary, prior to supporting the infantry in an attack against the fortified town of Gennep. Tom joined my troop at this point to replace Alan, injured two days beforehand in the Reichswald. When spare crew members were sent up to replace the squadron's casualties, Tom had asked his troop leader if he could join my troop in lieu of one of the replacements; the officer willingly agreed, and Johnny Walker was pleased to have a veteran rather than a rookie to replace the injured hull gunner/co-driver in our sergeant's tank.

I was in two minds about the matter: I was naturally pleased to have Tom with me, but we'd survived so far in different troops, and I wondered if we were tempting fate in the battles to come. There were only four of us left in the troop now of the original 15 who landed in Normandy: myself, Joe, Owen and Taffy. Whether his decision was wise or not, Tom was popular and the rest of my troop welcomed him with open arms.

So it was that, when the squadron set out early that afternoon to support the infantry attack on Gennep, the Dyson twins were in the same troop of tanks for the first time. One advantage was that we would be in sight of each other, rather than having the added worry while in action of wondering how the other one was faring in another part of the battlefield.

Our squadron advanced across country, the infantry dealing with a very determined enemy in strongpoints, houses and farm buildings, until we reached the outskirts of Gennep. On a hillside just outside the town, fate dealt our troop another cruel blow. We were advancing up a long, gentle slope with the infantry when the troop on our left reported shell fire coming from a wooded area the other side of the ridge. Johnny Walker brought our troop to a halt, then ran up the grassy slope and disappeared from our view. That was the last we saw of him.

After a while, during which we joked about Johnny trying to win the war on his own, we saw an infantry officer run down to Johnny's tank and speak to the operator in the turret. We were stunned to hear a message passed over the B-set to tell Sergeant Bradley that Johnny had been killed; decapitated, according to the infantry officer, by a shell from a tank or SP gun. Both Panther tanks and SP guns were sighted in the area, so it could have been either.

Sergeant Bradley took over the role of troop commander and relayed the tragic news to squadron HQ troop over the A-set. We carried on with the battle, taking part with our infantry in several fierce engagements, until the town of Gennep was captured.

Our squadron harboured overnight in the town, and it was then that we really began to feel the loss of our troop officer. With the battle for Gennep over, we had time to recall memories of our courageous leader, and his brilliant actions in all the battles from Falaise to Germany. He often took risks beyond the call of duty, as we could testify, and it seemed even more tragic that he should be struck down and killed so near the end of the war. Sergeant Bradley summed it up when he said, 'If anyone deserves a medal, Johnny does.'

His sentiments were echoed by us all, and were prophetic, as Johnny was eventually awarded the Military Cross.

Recalling Johnny's subdued behaviour the previous night, we

were all convinced he had a premonition of being killed in action. He had given me a photograph of himself in uniform, taken while he was an officer cadet at Sandhurst, and had written his address and telephone number on the back so we could meet after the war was over. Stifling my tears, I wrote on the back, 'my troop officer, Mr Walker, killed in action at Gennep'.

A new officer now took over command of 'Johnny's Troop': Captain Mike Hill. He was another swashbuckling type, with a small, neat moustache, and was a Normandy veteran to boot. Like Johnny, he too, was a Londoner. Gathering the crews together, he gave a little talk about what he expected of us, then said, 'I know how you must feel about Lieutenant Walker, lads. Some of you have been in action with him all the way from Normandy. He was a very brave man, and I know that he would want you to back me up in the coming battles as you backed him. I'm sure you will, and I feel proud to be taking over such a good fighting troop as this.' He could see in our faces that we would give our all for him, as we had done for Johnny.

Early on the morning of 14 February the squadron left Gennep to support the infantry in a drive towards the German town of Goch, some ten miles away. Mike Hill had briefed us on the formidable task ahead, pointing out on the map the enemy strongpoints between Gennep and the objective, including the Siegfried Line defences about three miles west of Goch.

We advanced parallel to the railway line for a few miles, meeting only token resistance from isolated pockets of enemy, but the real battles started as soon as we crossed the German border. From then onwards the Germans fought tenaciously for every inch of ground, and slowed up our advance to a crawl in the process. Even the houses were strongpoints, with enemy fire coming from slits above ground level in the reinforced cellars below. For seven days 107 Regiment battled its way through villages and farms, then the concrete bunkers and anti-tank hazards of the Siegfried Line, in support of the infantry. The 79th Armoured Division Funnies, the artillery, and RAF Typhoon aircraft were all called on at various stages to assist in clearing a pathway for us through the enemy fortifications.

155

It was a continuous, hard and weary slogging match, with both day and night attacks against well-fortified defence positions all the way. The weather was foul, with almost unceasing rain the whole time, and very cold. One cannot praise highly enough the courage, tenacity and sheer dogged determination of our 51st Highland Division infantry: time and time again we saw mud-caked Jocks advancing under fire, with many stopped in their tracks and falling, either wounded or dead. More heroics came from the medics, who were always up with the action attending to casualties.

Our troop had another courageous commander in Captain Mike Hill, and we took on many enemy positions with set-piece attacks. The squadron's advance culminated in an attack south of Goch on a night with very low cloud formation. This was ideal for searchlight beams to be reflected down to light up the area: 'Monty's Moonlight', as it was first named when it was used in the battles around Hill 112 in Normandy. It was a spectacular sight, with coloured tracer bullets from the tanks' Besa guns pouring in on enemy positions. After the infantry had routed the enemy and consolidated into defensive positions for the night, our squadron withdrew and harboured among a group of houses.

Before we could rest and have a meal, however, the supply trucks arrived and we replenished ammunition and fuel tanks. We also serviced the guns and tanks in readiness for an all-out attack to capture the southern part of Goch at a moment's notice. The town of Cleve had been captured on 16 February, and the 43rd Wessex Division had succeeded in taking the Goch escarpment and cutting the Kalcar - Goch road. This enabled 15th Scottish Division to launch an attack on the north of Goch on 18 February; and they had already taken this section by the time our infantry began to fight their way through the rubble-filled streets in the south of the town on 21 February.

As our troop accompanied the infantry, advancing further street by street, it was like Caen all over again. The buildings had been reduced to piles of rubble in recent saturation bombing by the RAF, which only helped to provide good cover for enemy snipers amidst the ruins. The drill was for our tanks to spray both sides of the street with a hail of bullets from our Besas, covering the Jocks as they leapfrogged along from building to building.

At one stage our troop stopped to let another troop take over for a further street advance by the infantry. We rested by a row of shops, or what was left of them, and some of the lads couldn't resist the opportunity to have a look and see if there was any loot to be had off the corpses of German soldiers lying around us. It was a forlorn hope, of course: the Jocks had been quick off the mark, as usual. I searched a still-warm body in a passageway, but the pockets of the dead German were empty, and any watch or rings had already been taken.

Mike Hill looked down from his perch in the turret of *Briton* and frowned on the grisly spectacle. 'You're a lot of vultures,' he shouted out. 'Have a little respect for the dead, even if they are Germans. And they could have been booby trapped.' He pointed to a 'Beware of booby traps' warning sign stuck up by the engineers over a poster of Hitler on a nearby wall, and we sheepishly returned to our tanks.

We waited there for about an hour, listening to the sounds of battle ahead and watching the activity around us: carriers taking back casualties; Royal Engineers putting up signs; ribald comments as some redcaps appeared; a wave and a special cheer from our lads as No 8 troop passed us going up to the front; Scottish infantry accompanying the troop, some with tin helmets and others with soft bobble hats. The 'if your name's on the bullet' fatalists disdained to wear helmets, and there were always some among the infantry in all our battles. The air was thick with clouds of dust, thrown up by the two-way traffic in the rubble-strewn streets, and smoke from fires in many of the ruined buildings. Goch, like Cleve, had been pulverised.

Whilst hanging about we had a brew up, and the hot tea warmed us and helped to clear the dust out of our mouths. Even amidst all the desecration and death, there were some lighter moments: Tom donned a top hat he found in the ruins, and clowned about with a walking stick in his hand. Captain Hill didn't seem to mind much, and was swift to guess that Tom was trying to impersonate W. C. Fields.

Shortly afterwards our troop was ordered forward again: the infantry was being impeded by a sizeable force of enemy barricaded inside a large factory. The Jocks were pinned down by heavy fire coming from many windows in the partly-demolished building. Mike Hill led us to a side street about a hundred yards short of the factory, then dismounted to consult with the infantry officer and make plans for an assault. Our orders were short and simple: our tanks were to enter the main street and fire HE shells at all the windows and doors in the factory, followed by a barrage from our Besa guns. Directly the tanks ceased fire, the infantry were to storm the place.

The target was split into three parts, and each tank would concentrate on one part only to achieve maximum effect. *Buzzard* was to take the near end, *Briton* the middle and *Brecon* the far end of the building. I watched Taffy's face crease into a smile, no doubt relishing the thought of pumping HE shells from the 75mm gun, and I made a quick check on the ammunition storage bin in the hull of the tank. There were still quite a few HEs left in the rack, so everything was ready to go and I could smoke a cigarette to help steady my nerves whilst waiting.

The noise of firing, from both our infantry and the enemy, echoed through the streets: sniper fire, rapid fire from a Spandau machine gun and the slower Bren machine guns of our infantry. We were given the order to advance, and I flicked my cigarette away, making tiny sparks as it hit a nearby wall. I closed the hatch just as Joe Whelan started the engine; we slowly moved forward to the main street and turned right. Taffy had already got one target lined up in his gun sight, and fired as we turned.

I was kept busy reloading the gun for Taffy to fire, with empty shell cases piling up around my feet as they were ejected from the breech block. The noise of the 75mm gun was deafening, and the smell of burnt explosives from ejected shells got down my throat as I reloaded. When Bob was satisfied we'd done enough with the HE, Taffy switched over to the turret Besa, joining with Owen on the hull Besa to send a spray of bullets at the near end of the factory.

I had a chance to look around, and peering through the periscope

I could see our other two tanks further up the street. Tom was in the sergeant's tank, *Brecon*, at the front, with the troop leader's tank a little way behind. Both were firing their 75mm guns, and blue tracer bullets from *Buzzard*'s Besas were making zig-zag lines through the smoke-laden air as they raked the building. When the other two tanks also switched over to their Besas, the tracer was a spectacular sight. We were ordered to cease firing, and the Jocks rushed in with bayonets fixed.

The Germans were amazingly adaptable: as the tremendous fire from our three tanks stopped, some desultory sniper fire came from parts of the factory, followed by a shot from a Panzerfaust through a ground floor window aimed at our tank. Fortunately for us the shot whizzed past *Buzzard*, but we dared not fire our turret Besa in retaliation because the Jocks were inside the building. Then a sharp-eyed Jock sniper put paid to the Panzerfaust gunner with a well-aimed shot from his position on the opposite side of the factory, and shortly afterwards all resistance inside the building crumbled.

The Jocks began to emerge from the main gates of the factory in groups, herding their prisoners before them. They were mainly paratroopers, and looked a sullen lot as they were led past our tank, giving Bob and me frosty stares as we watched them from the turret hatch. One of them even made an 'up yours' motion with his arms as he went by, but was immediately persuaded to put his hands over his head again after being rebuked by a Jock with the butt end of his rifle. The German winced audibly as the rifle was jabbed into his kidney region. The Jock spat some presumably nasty words at the paratrooper, then shouted something to us up in the turret, but couched in such a strong Scottish accent that the remark made no sense to Bob and me.

All our tension was released as we chatted amongst ourselves. Taffy was pleased with his shooting, and we decided to count the empty shell cases when we threw them out. The RAMC lads arrived on the scene and got busy tending the wounded, while Mike Hill ordered our tanks up to join him. Mike went to confer with the infantry commander, so some of us got out of our tanks to urinate against a wall by the side of a café. Tom joined me there, and when we had finished he took a look through the front of the half-demolished café. Standing there, marked only by a few bits of plaster fallen from the ceiling above, was a piano. The rest of the place was in a shambles, with empty bottles and broken china littering the floor and bar counter, and overturned tables and chairs lying in broken window glass and rubble. But the piano acted like a magnet on Tom, drawing him inside. Lifting the lid, he ran his fingers along the keys and commented that it was still in good condition. Just at that moment we heard a groaning sound coming from a room at the back of the café. We immediately fell silent for a few seconds, and drew our revolvers from our holsters, pointing them towards the open doorway. Tom indicated by a motion of his hand that he was going to investigate. He moved forward slowly to the doorway, pistol in hand, and took a quick peep around the corner. We looked on breathlessly, our revolvers at the ready, then relaxed as we saw Tom replace his gun.

The sight in the back room was rather sickening. Two German corpses were draped over the window ledge, and one wounded German lay on the floor near the window with part of his stomach hanging out. It looked as though he'd been bayoneted, and the other two shot up, by our infantry as the Germans tried to escape through the back window. Some of their personal papers and photographs were strewn around the floor, so the Jocks had obviously already been through their pockets.

The wounded man was in great pain and trying to say something, but a moaning sound was the only result. We came back out of the cafe, and I caught sight of a couple of RAMC lads stretchering off one of our Jocks. I shouted, 'There's a wounded Jerry in this café at the back.' Their reply was understandable: 'He'll have to wait then. We're looking after our own first.'

Mike Hill came back to the troop with good news: reports were coming through that the enemy had begun to withdraw out of the town, and the battle for Goch was over. It was some of the stiffest fighting I had seen, and there were heavy casualties on both sides. Among my souvenirs are several photographs of a German paratroop officer which I found strewn around his dead body in a doorway that morning. Some were portrait photos, others taken with civilians, but I wrote 'Goch, 22/2/45' on the back of each picture. Our squadron pulled out of the town the following morning.

Chapter 15

After the Battle

There was nothing worth taking from the ruins of Goch, but the looting began later on that day when we started to live off the land. Farms were a prime target, and my diary records the meals we enjoyed: '22 February. Had a good dinner on chicken and ham. Plenty of food here. 23 February. Dinner of turkey, goose and ham. 24 February. Goose and chicken and ham. Boy are we living!'

After weeks of compo rations we were ready to gorge ourselves on produce that was there for the taking. Farmers and farmworkers made themselves scarce when we descended upon them like a swarm of locusts; although the birds showed a marked reluctance to submit voluntarily to having their necks wrung, and forced us to tear after them hurling abuse and making more noise than our squawking prey. But we were now conquerors and not liberators, as had been the case in the other countries through which we had fought. Our officers turned a blind eye to the looting and, in some instances, took an active part.

I was surprised to receive a hand-delivered letter from Mini, the girl I met at Tongres. She had given it to a chap in our squadron when he spent his leave with the family who billeted him in their home while the regiment was there. It was written by this lad in good English, with little bits by Mini herself, and enclosed two photographs of her. I'd been foraging for poultry and was covered in feathers, as were Tom and the other lads in our troop, when we returned to our tanks and the lad came up with the letter. He handed it to me with a grin, and said in a loud voice for all to hear, 'so you're going to marry Mini then!'

I dropped the dead chicken I was holding and opened the letter. Disbelief showed on my face as I read that she hoped to become Mrs Dyson. 'That's what your mock wedding stunt has done,' I chuckled, handing the letter to Tom. Very soon the whole squadron assumed there was a wedding in the offing, and for the next few days I was showered with congratulations.

Following the capture of Goch, our squadron was granted a rest on 27 February. We'd been in continuous action for 20 days against a fanatical enemy, who at all times had the advantage of fighting from well-built bunkers and strongpoints, so we'd earned our break the hard way. We withdrew from the front line and harboured in a field near Grafenthal: the fighting was over for us for the time being. But other British and Canadian forces joined the US Ninth Army to squeeze the pocket of Germans on this side of the Rhine. The enemy had the choice of withdrawing across the Rhine, or losing thousands more in a bloody fight to defend their territory with their backs to the river.

It was a nice change for us to sit back and follow the course of the battle over the radio, instead of being involved at the sharp end. We decided to celebrate. Tom suggested to our troop leader that we throw a big party for the squadron, hinting that he knew where he could get a piano to make it a right old ding-dong. Mike Hill was not averse to our looting (other than from dead bodies), and readily gave his permission for Sergeant Bradley's crew to take their tank out on a trial run, ostensibly to test it after some engine maintenance. They went first to a farm and bagged 14 chickens and a pig, then carried on into Goch to the café where Tom had seen the piano. To his delight it was still there, and soon loaded onto their tank. The rest of our squadron were astonished to see a piano on the back of a Churchill tank, as were the many onlookers who gazed at the spectacle in disbelief on the way back from Goch.

In no time at all the piano was unloaded at our troop's position on the edge of the field, and Tom was trying out a few tunes. The whole troop got busy plucking chickens in readiness for the

163

cooking pot – a large galvanised iron bath – while a butcher in the squadron was employed to deal with the pig, which met its end with a couple of bullets through the head from Tom's revolver. The carcass was soon ready, and hung up on a tree after Tom had shaved its bristles off with an open razor he intended taking home to Dad, a devotee of the cut-throat.

I have a photograph of the troop, including Captain Hill, plucking chickens with the pig's carcass hanging up on one of the trees behind us. Tom is in the foreground holding up the pig's head by its ears: he had bagged it, and he claimed the privilege. 'What a pity we haven't got a taxidermist in the squadron, Dyson T.,' commented Mike Hill. 'That would be a lovely trophy for you, stuffed and hung on your wall at home.'

Soon the chickens were plucked clean, with the wind blowing feathers all over the place, and we started a huge fire ready to boil the chickens and pork in the bath. That night B Squadron held its own victory celebrations to mark the end of the Battle of the Reichswald Forest. There were ample helpings of pork, poultry and vegetables, washed down with unlimited quantities of looted booze. With Tom on the piano, Jock Gould on trumpet, Tommy Reilly on guitar and me on the violin, the party went on until the early hours of the morning. The squadron officers joined the men in the festivities, and rank was temporarily put in the background. But my trusty old violin played its last farewell that night: someone accidentally pushed in the bridge and cracked the body of the instrument as it lay on top of the piano. Someone, they joked, who couldn't stand the sound of it!

After the party we were brought down to earth with a bang the next morning: near panic set in with the officers when they heard General Horrocks was to pay us a visit at midday. The massed bands and pipes of the 51st Highland Division were also to descend upon us, to rehearse for a Grand Victory Parade at the end of the week to be attended by the Prime Minister, Winston Churchill, and C-in-C Montgomery. Hangovers were soon cured in a hectic site clean-up, and a quick bash at the long forgotten spit-and-polish routine. Surprisingly, after a period of seemingly disorganised chaos, we were all spick and span and standing by our battle-scarred but clean tanks when the general arrived. Our natural aversion to bull was subjugated to our desire to prove ourselves worthy of the great honour bestowed on the regiment.

General Horrocks, the commander of 30 Corps, stopped by our troop on his tour of inspection and pointed to something that caught his eye in the background: the smoke-blackened galvanised iron bath, hanging up on a tree. He went behind our tanks to take a closer look, accompanied by our CO and Captain Hill, with SSM Braybrook in tow looking a little apprehensive. He needn't have worried: our straining ears could hear voices and peals of laughter, after which the general reappeared and carried on with the inspection. Mike Hill told us later that the general tapped his stick on the bath and speculated on the unlikelihood of any troops taking an outside wash in this weather. Then he looked at the chicken feathers scattered around, and suggested there was more than one use for a bath, adding that he too had been enjoying some rich fare in the past few days!

The air was filled with the sound of bagpipes and drums as the bands rehearsed for the victory parade, while signallers installed a microphone on a stage erected by the engineers, and a number of loudspeakers on the perimeter of our large field. For the next few days everyone was hard at it, preparing for the big day. Men, tanks and equipment underwent a transformation, from scruffy, dirty and battle-worn to smart, best battle-dressed soldiers and clean tanks with freshly-painted yellow names on their sides. The site too was clean, with so much whitewash on inanimate objects everywhere that one had the feeling of being back at Catterick rather than in Germany.

It was all worthwhile in the end, as the parade was a most memorable occasion. Sunday 4 March dawned bright and dry, with the Churchills of 107 Regiment RAC lined up around the field perimeter and representatives from various units of 51st Highland Division assembled in their allotted positions. The massed bands and pipes were all ready. After a longish wait the VIPs arrived in all their splendour: Winston Churchill; Generals Lord Alanbrooke and Hastings Ismay (CIGS and Chief of Staff to the Minister of Defence respectively); Field Marshal Montgomery;

General Dempsey, commander of the British Second Army; General Frank Simpson; and General Horrocks, who had arrived before the VIPs and looked as if he had just dashed in from the front line wearing his favourite bush jacket.

The top brass were escorted to the stage, and as soon as they were settled in the ceremony began. The bands and pipes played stirring music, marching and counter-marching in perfect unison. It was an emotional and colourful spectacle as the Scots pipers in their kilts marched to the skirl of the pipes, proud as peacocks in front of Winston Churchill; and a perfect setting for the rousing speech, typically Churchillian in its punctuation and delivery, given to the troops by the Prime Minister. It sent our pulses racing as we listened, spellbound, to the oratory.

Churchill seemed to relish the historical occasion he'd come to celebrate: he was going to take the salute at a military parade on German soil to mark our victory in the Battle of the Reichswald, and he could hardly contain his enthusiasm! I almost expected him to slap his thigh and do a little jig, as Hitler did when his troops captured Paris in 1940. A beaming smile lit up the face of the old warhorse as he stood talking to Monty and the other generals, walking stick in one hand and a cigar in the other, and gesticulating with both. The Prime Minister was enjoying himself, but he was also visibly moved, and the emotion came through over the loudspeakers as he launched into his speech.

He lavished praise on us for achieving the first victory on German territory, but noted that the Battle of the Reichswald Forest and the capture of Cleve and Goch by 30th Corps, under the command of General Horrocks, had only been won with a great sacrifice in lives.

Pausing a few seconds, as if overcome with emotion, he carried on, 'We shall remember them! We pray for their souls and their families at home. Britain has fought its way back from the dark days following the evacuation of our forces in Dunkirk, when we stood alone against the military might of Hitler and his Nazi regime. We now have our feet planted firmly on German soil and we, together with our allies, are now poised to thrust our way across the Rhine and drive through the plains of

166

Germany, to plunge the dagger into the heart of Hitler's Nazi Reich!'

When Churchill had finished his speech, the lads responded so vociferously to the three cheers called for by Monty that we drowned the sound of gunfire in the distance. No one who witnessed this memorable event will ever forget the splendour of it all: it was ingrained in our minds for evermore. Sir Brian Horrocks even refers to the occasion in his book *Corps Commander*, published in 1977, 32 years after the event.

My crowning moment on that unforgettable day, the icing on my cake, came as the VIPs were departing: the limousine carrying Churchill got bogged down in mud as it approached the field's exit, just by our troop of tanks. We watched as the driver tried to get out of the rut, but the car's wheels kept spinning round aimlessly each time he revved up the engine, so Mike Hill ordered us to give a helping hand. We had lots of experience in extricating vehicles stuck in mud, and this one was child's play to us: with a heave from the combined weight of our troop, we soon had the limousine on its way with its famous passenger.

I was able to get a close-up look at the great man, sitting in the rear offside seat with Lord Alanbrooke beside him, as I was on that side of the car and could see Churchill watching us through the window. He looked magnificent in his resplendent army uniform and cap, with a smile like a Cheshire cat on his face as he gave us a little wave with a hand clutching a lighted cigar about a foot long.

Three days after the victory parade I was ordered to see our CO. The SSM marched me into the large tent which served as squadron HQ, and the CO informed me that both the late Lieutenant Walker and Captain Hill had recommended me for promotion. He had decided to promote me to the rank of lance-corporal there and then. Thanking him, I went to the stores truck to collect my stripes, then returned to my troop with the news. There was the inevitable jocular ribbing from Tom and the others as I busied myself sewing the stripes onto my sleeves.

On 8 March we heard that the US 9th Armoured Division had crossed the Rhine over the railway bridge at Remagen. The

167

Germans had apparently failed in their attempts to blow up the bridge, and a small force of Americans succeeded in fighting their way over to the east bank of the river, then held on until the main force crossed the next morning. By 10 March all German resistance had ceased on the west bank of the Rhine, and the enemy withdrew across the river. But the Reichswald battle was won at a very high cost: from 8 February to 10 March the First Canadian Army suffered 15,634 casualties, of which nearly two-thirds were British troops of 30 Corps. The German losses were estimated at 22,000, with a further 22,000 taken prisoner.

On 11 March our regiment was withdrawn to rest and refit. Tom played a last tune on the piano before it had to be abandoned, and the lads gathered round to join in the chorus of 'Goodbyee, goodbyee' before mounting our tanks and driving off. Although we could not know it, this was our swan song; apart from minor skirmishes later on, the 34th Tank Brigade fought the last of its battles in the Reichswald.

As our tanks crossed the German border and drove through the Dutch villages, we were given a great reception all the way. We crossed the River Maas at Venlo and stayed the night at Blerick, the scene of one of our earlier battles. The following day, 12 March, we reached our destination: Liest army barracks!

It was unbelievable, really. We'd been released from the battlefield, after a month's hard fighting under the most gruelling conditions, supposedly for a rest. It had mattered not one jot how you dressed, officers included, and the only criteria were the fighting qualities of the men themselves. Yet here we were being subjected to the discipline of an army barracks, with endless spit-and-polish at the whim of some brass hat. The SSM, whose duty it was to ensure a high level of bull, came in for some scathing criticism from the lads. Our only consolation was the luxury of beds in the comparative comfort of a barrack room, instead of sleeping rough wherever we could in the freezing cold as we'd been doing since leaving Oirschot at the beginning of February.

Entertainment was provided for us in the concert hall at Liest barracks: a Belgian concert party and an ENSA party both staged thoroughly enjoyable shows. Another bonus was female company to be had in the nearby town of Deurne; although the beer in the cafés there, as I noted in my diary, was 'putrid'. But it was like Catterick all over again, assembling on parade in the barracks square for inspection by the CO. After such a long period without our feet touching a parade ground, one would have expected our drill movements to be well below par, but, like riding a bike, once learned never forgotten. Donk was even heard paying us a compliment after the event - rare praise from that quarter.

Our troops were transformed in just a few days: from looking like scarecrows when we arrived on Monday, to one of the smartest bodies of men ever to grace a barrack square on the Saturday. It was a rehearsal for another full-scale parade on 20 March, to present awards for gallantry in the field. We did wonder what some of the recipients had done to deserve them; even Sir Brian Horrocks comments in his book that 'The medals came up with the rations'. Most of the awards were well justified, and in some instances were verified by witnesses to the actions given in the citations, as with the posthumous MC awarded to Johnny Walker. But, setting aside sour grapes on the part of a few lads, there was little doubt that some of the medals seemed to be handed out to make up the quota in the regimental allotment, and surprised even those who received them.

An air of excitement pervaded the barracks on 24 March as we watched hundreds of gliders soaring above our heads towards the east bank of the Rhine. Units of the 51st Highland Division had forced a crossing of the river at Wesel, and the assault across the Rhine was under way. The US Third Army had also captured a bridge at Oppenheim, and secured a bridgehead on the east bank. It was cause for elation, as we knew we would soon be back in action. We felt like caged birds in the confines of barracks, and yearned for the freedom of the countryside. Our wishes came true on 30 March, when the regiment was put under orders to move.

Chapter 16

Across the Rhine

Before the regiment left Deurne, every man was given a letter from Monty on the subject of non-fraternisation, and the attitude we should adopt towards the German people. It was in the shape of a small folded card, suitable to be kept handy in a breast pocket, and included instructions such as, 'You must keep clear of Germans, man, woman and child, unless you meet them in the course of duty. You must not walk out with them, or shake hands, or make them gifts or take gifts from them. You must not play games with them or share any social event with them. In short, you must not fraternise with Germans at all.'

We'd hardly seen a civilian in the path of our battles in Germany, so the issue of non-fraternisation had yet to be tested. The notable exception was a grizzled old Jerry with a huge grey moustache, dressed in what appeared to be an old, navy blue railway uniform and peak cap. We met him on a farm we were raiding, and thought he looked like a relic of the First World War. He seemed, by his agitated manner, to be objecting to us catching and wringing the necks of some poultry, but he wouldn't 'fuck orf', as repeatedly requested by the lads. To keep him quiet, Tom wrote out a chitty as a receipt for the birds, penning the signature of Colonel Charlie Chaplin. He gave this to the old Kraut, who glanced at it and then ambled off back into the farmhouse clutching the piece of paper, seemingly satisfied with its authenticity. Brought up under the disciplines of Kaiser Bill and totalitarian Nazism, any piece of paper with a signature attached would seem official to the old German, and was to be accepted without question.

We were like a lot of schoolboys at the end of term as we stowed equipment away in our tanks and moved out of the barracks on 30 March. Our journey took us back across the Maas and into Germany again. The roads leading to the Rhine were packed with transport waiting to cross, and it was a slow process. The area for miles around was chock-a-block with store dumps and equipment and reminded one of the beachhead area of Normandy. When the squadron harboured overnight we were all chuffed to get back to the nomadic life once more. Up went the bivouacs, and we gathered in our troop 'families' around the camp fire, brewing up at intervals and chain-smoking until it was time to get our heads down.

The following morning our tanks crossed over the beautiful, fast-flowing Rhine at Wesel on a bridge erected by the engineers. It was a wonderful experience, as the river is about two hundred yards wide from bank to bank at this point. Wesel was in complete ruins, having been 'taken out' by massive air raids and artillery barrages prior to assault by our forces. As we drove along we could see airborne troop gliders all over the place, many totally wrecked.

We stopped at a village a few miles from Wesel, where for the first time we saw a few civilians - all were either old or very young. It was our first occasion to heed the warning on non-fraternisation. The Germans looked such a pathetic lot, watching in silence as we refuelled the tanks. But their curiosity was reciprocated, and the children ignited a tiny spark of sympathy in us, even though they were Germans. First one, then another, of the lads tried surreptitiously to give chocolate or sweets to the kids; the rest followed suit, and our officers turned a blind eye.

The British soldier, wherever he may be, has a soft heart where children are concerned, even for the children of our enemies. This wave of sympathy for the 'little innocents' caught up in the retribution being exacted on the German population was not confined to the lower ranks. Even Sir Brian Horrocks, the commander of 30 Corps, organised a party for 150 German children at his HQ. He was subjected to scathing criticism in the press at the time, and Monty was furious, but Horrocks wrote later that Nelson was not the only commander with a blind eye!

On 2 April our squadron was despatched to Dinghem to take over the protection of Second Army HQ. Armoured units had swanned through the Westphalian plain, bypassing many isolated groups of diehard enemy, and these were a threat which had to be countered. That was now our responsibility, so for the rest of the week we were moved about like chess pieces as reports came in of spasmodic resistance here and there. It never amounted to much: the sight of our tanks was enough to quell the odd pockets of enemy, who were so dispirited that, as we had found at Falaise, they almost begged to be taken into captivity.

Our travels took us to the towns of Bocholt, Bochum (both bombed flat, as I noted in my diary), Neuenkirchen and Burgsteinfurt, amongst others. I must admit that we did our share of looting, restricted only by our capacity to carry the spoils. Jock Gould managed to get hold of a violin for me, so I was back in business with the musical group when next the opportunity arose.

We arrived in Osnabruck, or what was left of it, on 9 April, where my troop had the great honour of being assigned to take over responsibility for the personal protection of General Sir Miles Dempsey at his HQ in a field outside the town. It was the scene of much activity, with many visitors calling to see the commander of the British Second Army: C-in-C Montgomery visited on the first day we were there. The field marshal looked uncharacteristically stern-faced as he alighted from his transport and strode purposefully into his meeting with Dempsey.

On the day after we arrived at HQ, we discovered some very distinguished neighbours living in a tent only a few yards from where our troop was parked: the senior Commando officers, Lord Lovat and General Sturges. His Lordship was quite a jolly man, with not a bit of 'side' about him whatsoever. Both he and General Sturges showed interest in our battle-scarred Churchills, engaging Captain Hill in discussion of 107 Regiment's battles and talking to our lads in general. They seemed to enjoy our banter.

We moved with HQ to Schledehausen on 11 April, and on to another site near the town of Minden the following day.

Everybody was stunned to hear of the death of President Roosevelt: it was especially sad that this great American, who had helped Britain in her hour of need and played a leading role in the fight against tyranny, should pass away on the eve of victory.

At Roosevelt's memorial service in St Paul's Cathedral a few days later, which was broadcast to the whole world, many tributes were paid to this man for whom the British people had a very special affection. In a broadcast from the steps of the cathedral, that special feeling was conveyed on behalf of ordinary people by Mrs Margaret Dyson. The BBC had chosen and rehearsed her for the part at short notice, and it was a proud moment indeed for my mother and the Dyson family.

As the general's bodyguard, we noted the comings and goings of VIPs. General Dempsey was visited in mid-April by both General Horrocks and General Neil Ritchie; presumably to discuss which of the two corps commanders was to mount the assault on the town of Bremen.

We were all shocked when we received eye-witness accounts of the horrors found by the troops liberating Belsen concentration camp on 15 April. The thousands of dead bodies and living skeletons at death's door discovered there were an affront to humanity, and testimony to the atrocities perpetrated by the SS camp guards, male and female, under an inhuman SS camp commander, Josef Kramer. First-hand reports of decaying corpses piled in heaps all over the compound, and starvation and disease rife amongst the inmates, were sickening to hear.

On 17 April Captain Hill was awarded the French Croix de Guerre, for outstanding merit in the battles at Hill 112 in Normandy. The lads were very pleased for him, and a bottle of schnapps was immediately produced to drink a toast to mark the occasion.

Things were getting pretty cushy for us. During the daylight hours we would sally forth on assignment, flushing out isolated groups of enemy here and there, or protecting a military supply convoy, handing over to another tank troop at the next roadblock. Streaming back down the roads were German civilians, with their belongings in suitcases, wheelbarrows, prams and horse-drawn

173

carts. Unarmed groups of shabbily-dressed enemy soldiers shambled along, looking downcast and pleading to be taken to a POW camp by any of us who troubled to listen. There were also foreign displaced persons, liberated by our troops, wandering along seeking food and shelter with the British in special camps provided for them.

On the way back from one of these operations, we towed a damaged and abandoned Bren gun carrier to our camp. The lads thought it would be useful to hold any excess baggage (ie. loot!), but Tom had other ideas. Sitting round the camp fire that night, frying some eggs we'd filched from a farm, the idea took shape: why shouldn't we produce our own eggs? Sergeant Bradley was doubtful, and removed the pipe from his mouth to point the stem at Tom, but Tom triumphantly went on to outline his plan. 'We'll get some chickens, and keep them in the carrier for laying.'

Mike Hill raised no objection when permission was sought from him, and next day the plan was put into operation. The sergeant's crew left camp to go on safari in *Brecon* very early in the morning, towing the carrier with the name *Bethnal Green* painted in yellow on its sides (conforming with the squadron identity of names beginning with 'B', Tom suggested naming the carrier after our London borough). They returned in triumph, towing a travelling chicken coop in the shape of the carrier. It had a bed of straw, the top was covered with chicken wire, and there was a load of noisy hens inside.

General Sir Miles Dempsey turned a blind eye to this phenomenon. He went past our troop site with some staff officers one day, busily engaged in conversation, and glanced at the carrier as he returned our salute. Like the old 'double take' in films, he suddenly stopped and came back in disbelief to take a closer look. He stood by the side of *Bethnal Green*, watching the chickens pecking away at some scraps we had thrown to them, smiled a little, then diplomatically passed on again to resume his discussion with the officers.

My diary told me it was Hitler's birthday on 20 April. The Russians were in the outskirts of Berlin, and I wrote 'Happy Birthday, Adolf?' in the space for that day. The following day we were on red alert continuously until a pocket of enemy near us was wiped out, with 4,000 prisoners taken, plus tanks and guns.

There were numerous actions to deal with pockets of enemy all over the place, bypassed in the rapid advance of the armoured units. With no lines of communication left the enemy was disorientated: defeat for Germany was staring them in the face. The majority recognised the folly of continuing the fight and laid down their arms, but for the SS it was a battle to the finish. One such enemy force was holding out in the forest of Munster, so our troops rejoined the squadron to help flush them out. The chickens were consigned to the pot before we left, poor things, after having dutifully supplied us with eggs. SSM Braybrook might have suffered a heart attack if we'd taken them with us.

At first light on 27 April our troop left Second Army HQ and eventually met up with our squadron at the designated rendezvous. No one relished going into action at this late stage in the game; particularly Tom and I, as we were due to go on leave within a few days. Anyway, off we went and the squadron joined the infantry in combing the Munster forest. Up and down the forest rides we drove, firing our Besas into the woods as directed by the trusty old footsloggers. It was a doddle compared to the Reichswald, and by mid-afternoon the enemy succumbed. Not one of our tanks had fired a shell from a 75mm gun, much to the chagrin of Taffy. He felt cheated!

As some of the prisoners were escorted back past our tanks they gave us the German equivalent of 'up yours' with their arms, defiant to the end. Their comrades, lying in the woods either dead or wounded, were unfortunate to have become casualties in this needless last-ditch action against overwhelming odds.

Although we couldn't foresee it at the time, the Churchill tanks of B Squadron, 107 Regiment RAC fought their last engagement there in the forest of Munster. Later that day came news of the capture of Bremen by units of 30 Corps, followed by the great news that the Americans had met up with Russian troops at Torgau on the River Elbe, south of Berlin. It was clear that it could now be only weeks, if not days, before the unconditional surrender of Germany.

Our troop returned to Second Army HQ, which was constantly moving camp to shorten the lines of communication. By 2 May we were at Fallingbostel, near Soltau, where Tom and I bade farewell to the lads and started on our journey for UK leave. We had so much loot to take home to the family that we would have been glad of a pack mule to carry it, and our pockets were lined with cash from black market deals. We would change our 'dirty' money into clean English currency to pay for a victory celebration with the family in Bethnal Green.

Just before we left our troop, the Dyson twins performed one last little ceremony. I hunted in my metal ammunition case and found the two bottles of pale ale I had bought at the pub in Fareham just prior to embarking on the LCT taking our troop to Normandy. I'd vowed then that if Tom and I survived to see the end of the war we would drink these in a victory toast.

The war in Europe was now all over bar the shouting: Hitler was reported to be dead; Mussolini and his mistress Clara Petacci had been executed by Italian partisans on 28 April. So, with the rest of the troop gathered round, I handed Tom one of the bottles. He removed the crown cork top and poured beer into his enamel mug, while I did the same. Then we clicked our mugs and drank the toast to our survival, and to victory. The whole troop, led by Mike Hill, responded by raising their mugs of schnapps, and wished us a safe journey back to London. 'Don't forget to come back,' Mike quipped. 'Things could never be the same without the Dyson twins.'

As we waved goodbye, it struck me again that out of the original 15 who landed in Normandy with me, only three were left: Joe, Taffy and Owen. We had fought in every battle from the Normandy beaches to the recent action in the forest of Munster. Of the three tanks, only *Buzzard* had survived without being replaced.

Chapter 17

Home on Leave

At regimental HQ we joined the rest of the UK leave party and were transported to a transit camp, bulging at the seams with hundreds of others awaiting their turn to be processed onto the next stage homewards. Everyone was hoping, like Tom and I, to get home in time to celebrate VE Day, and we got very frustrated at the delays. It took days to move us in stages to camps along the route, amidst scenes of the utmost chaos.

The roads were chock-a-block with pedestrians and traffic, and there were long lines of enemy soldiers marching westwards. Thousands and thousands of them slouched along, having lain down their arms to seek refuge in POW camps, unkempt, hungry and totally downcast at the terrible fate that had befallen the once-mighty Germany. Many were elderly men and young boys, drafted in towards the end of the war. There were also refugees and slave labourers, all streaming along the roads with their prized personal possessions. This movement of pitiful humanity was shepherded by small groups of British infantry, who did their best to clear the roads and allow long army convoys through.

It took five days under these conditions to get back across the Rhine to a transit camp at Gennep, the town we had assisted the infantry to capture in February. It brought back unhappy memories of Lieutenant Johnny Walker, killed in that battle.

On the homeward journey we followed radio reports of the dramatic events in the last days of war with Germany. We were at a transit camp on 7 May when we heard that Germany had signed an unconditional surrender. Everybody in the camp went bonkers celebrating the occasion. It was a wonderful feeling: peace in Europe at last, officially! We would have loved to celebrate this great event with our own mates, but at least Tom and I were together at the end.

Our one great desire now was to get home for VE Day. It looked as though we could make it as we left Gennep on 7 May, but we only got as far as Turnhout, in Belgium, before being shunted into yet another transit camp for the night. Tom grumbled as we bustled among the crowds queuing at the Naafi bars for drinks, and I tried to console him by pointing out that we would reach Calais the next day, from where it was only an hour's boat crossing.

My optimism proved to be wishful thinking: we reached Calais on 8 May, the date Churchill had designated VE Day, but we were among thousands waiting their turn to embark on boats for the short trip across the Strait of Dover. Frustration mounted as time went by and we watched ships crammed to overflowing sail away, hoping to get the next one. But at the end of the day the 'next one' was to sail the following morning, and we didn't make it after all.

We followed other lads going to drown their disappointment in a binge at the local cafés: the ladies of the brothels were delighted, as they did a roaring trade among many of those who missed the last boat home that day. The majority were content to limit themselves to boozing and merriment, and that was how Tom and I celebrated the end of almost six years of bitter struggle against Germany.

Next day, after downing a few 'hairs of the dog', we eventually boarded our ship and left Calais docks. We were all in a happy mood, and the white cliffs of Dover were a most welcome sight as we steamed ever nearer to the coast before docking at Folkestone. When we were told we would be subject to customs inspection, quite a few men dumped bulky or expensive loot overboard rather than face the consequences if the officials declined to turn a blind eye to the obvious. Tom and I got straight through customs with the things in our kitbags intact, however, and joined the crowds heading towards the London train. It was packed out, with the unlucky ones crowded in the corridors to stand all the way.

As the train steamed out of the station, Tom and I lit a cigarette each and sat back to enjoy the last leg of our journey. It had been eight boring, tiring days since we left our unit in Germany, but it was now only a matter of hours before we knocked on the door at home. I reflected that it was just as well our nine days' UK leave started from the day of our arrival in England, otherwise we'd have to go straight back again!

We caught a bus from Bank to Bethnal Green Road. It was lovely to pass all the familiar landmarks, the pubs, the shops and the market stalls. We rang the bell at our door at precisely 17.30 hours.

Home at last! Phyllis, who had opened the window on the top floor landing to see who was at the door, nearly fell out in her excitement at seeing us standing there. We heard her scream, followed by the pounding of feet as she tore down several flights of stairs to open the door. She could hardly contain herself as she hugged us both in turn, quickly followed by Eileen, who was weeping with joy. We all trooped upstairs, the girls babbling away with rapid fire questions, and went to greet Mum and Dad with a little less excitement but just as much feeling. A hug from Mum and a handshake from Dad said it all.

Mum went out into the kitchen to make a pot of tea while Tom and I put our things in my bedroom. He would be sharing with me now his divorce proceedings were in motion. Over tea we had the whole family in fits of laughter as we recounted some of the hilarious things we'd got up to, although everyone was sad that we hadn't arrived in time for VE Day. The big moment came when Tom and I took the goodies out of our kitbags, with the air of magicians pulling rabbits from top hats: watches, bits of jewellery, powder compacts, fine china and glassware, a roll of dress material, and an ornate German beer mug with a pewter lift-up lid as a special present for Dad. It had the name *Monchengladbach* on its decorated surface, and Dad was chuffed with this, as well as a silver pocket watch and chain, cuff links, and the open razor Tom had used to shave the pig.

179

We ate fish and chips that evening, which we had missed since going abroad, and they tasted absolutely scrumptious. Then it was down to the Cornwallis for plenty of drinks all round. For the first time since the blackout had been imposed, Tom and I saw Bethnal Green with the lights on - a lovely sight!

The next day we took the family up to the West End to join the celebrating crowds and see a show. We mingled with civilians and forces of all nationalities in Trafalgar Square, and everyone was in high spirits. Some extroverts were cavorting about in the fountains, pulling girls in with them; street sellers were doing a roaring trade in paper hats and streamers. It was one big party. Along Oxford Street the big stores were decked with bunting and flying flags of all nations. Piccadilly Circus had been taken over by the Yanks.

Tom and I went on endless pub crawls with our mates that leave, in both the East End and West End. With celebrations going on everywhere it was no wonder the pubs started to run dry - but not before we stocked up with enough booze for two marvellous Saturday night parties. We got two complete weekends in our leave rather than one thanks to rumours among troops in the West End bars, who said it wasn't too difficult to get an extension of leave. Now the war with Germany was over, an excuse as weak as 'the cat's had kittens' was apparently sufficient reason to be given a few extra days; and so we found when our leave expired on 17 May, and we were granted three extra days by a sympathetic RTO at Victoria in response to our concocted tale of a crisis at home. I suspect the officer didn't believe a word of it!

On Friday, the third day of our leave, we had a reunion with our eldest sister, Maggie. She came over with Albert, her husband, and young Albie, to spend the day with us. There were tears of joy again as Maggie hugged and kissed us in turn, and they were pleased with their presents. Young Albie was the most thrilled, when I gave him the German army belt with the eagle buckle I'd promised to bring home for him. Maggie and Albert came up both weekends for our big parties; as did Freddie Robinson, Phyllis's RAF flying officer fiancé, who seemed to get leave passes at will.

One unforgettable incident during this leave concerns audacity and enterprise in coping with the beer shortage. We were out on a pub crawl at the height of the drought with Con, a mate of ours, and found pub after pub closed with 'sold out' notices outside. Our tongues were hanging out when Tom spotted Mann Crossman & Paulin's brewery, staring at it with the look of a man dying of thirst discovering a desert oasis. He went through the brewery entrance, with Con and I following close behind.

A man appeared from a little office just inside the gateway and tried to block our path with his arms outstretched. As this was Tom's idea, Con and I were content to let him do the talking. Tom politely asked for a drink, but the man responded with incredulous sneers and pointed to a water tap on the yard, behaving as though a brewery was the last place to find beer, although his pot belly must have been caused by drinking too much of the stuff. He suggested that we try a pub, but Tom informed him that we already had - plenty! - with no luck. It was hard on men just returned from fighting in Germany, we said, let alone one just out of a POW camp (Con had been captured at Arnhem, and only recently released by the Germans).

Before I could add anything further, the man adopted a sympathetic attitude. 'Oh well, in that case I'll see what I can do.' Bidding us to follow him, he went into the office and we heard him speaking on the telephone. 'Joe, there's a couple of tank men here on leave from Germany, and a paratrooper just released from a German prison camp. D'ya fink you can spare 'em a drink? Yus, here at the gate. Rightio then. I'll tell 'em.'

He reappeared with a smile of satisfaction on his face, and gave us the thumbs up sign. 'You'll be OK now, lads. Hang on a bit and Joe will be up in 'arf a mo'.'

Joe appeared shortly, in the shape of a heavily-built, bald-headed man with a large moustache, wearing a white warehouse coat. He greeted us with a smile. 'So you've just come back from Germany, eh, lads? Well you deserve the freedom of the brewery, I say.' He took us through the yard and into the brewery, passing some huge vats, and ushered us into a little office. Workers in the

181

plant stared in curiosity as we passed by, and must have wondered what was going on. What were the army doing here?

'Make yourselves at home, lads, and I'll go and get you some beer,' said Joe as he left us. 'But don't spread it around, otherwise we'll have the whole flippin' army dropping in for a pint!' A satisfied grin lit up Tom's face in anticipation of a dream fulfilled: finding himself inside a brewery with an unlimited supply of beer. It was only two weeks since we'd been fighting in the forest of Munster, yet it seemed a long way away. Joe came back with a huge pewter jug filled to the top with beer, followed by another man holding some tankards. Joe filled the tankards and handed them round, and we got stuck into a long boozing session with him and his colleague. The more we told them of our war exploits, the quicker the tankards of beer went down and the merrier we became. It was an unforgettable experience.

We were all well away when Joe took us back through the plant again, and I found myself holding onto the pipework for support as I staggered along. Joe shook our hands and wished us good luck as we departed. We walked a little unsteadily along Whitechapel Road, in a jolly and boisterous mood, and were soon passing Truman Hanbury & Buxton's brewery. I suggested to the others that we try again, but Con responded by spewing up into the gutter. Perhaps his stomach was weakened by his spell in captivity, or the thought of another boozing session so soon after the last one made him sick. I myself needed a long rest that day before I could face another pint, but when Dad heard of our escapade he was green with envy!

At the end of our momentous leave, I wrote in my diary: 'spent £70 on this leave but well worth it.' As this was the equivalent of 18 weeks' wages for the average civilian at that time, it was a lot of money to spend in just 12 days.

Tom and I caught the 11pm Victoria – Folkestone train on 20 May, joining hundreds of others with long faces returning from leave. By the following day we had rejoined our unit at Nordwalde, near Munster. I remarked to Tom that, typically, it took eight days for them to get us home but only two days to get us back again!

Chapter 18

Counting the Cost

After crossing the Rhine on our way back to our unit we had
passed through the ruined towns of Duisberg, Essen, Bochum and
Dortmund, completely devastated by RAF and USAAF bombing
raids. I felt a twinge of pity as I saw the civilians, mainly old
people and kids, all doing their best to cope with the aftermath
of Germany's crushing defeat. One couldn't fail to have sympathy
for the children: the flaxen-haired young girls, with long plaits
hanging down their backs, would melt a heart of stone. I reminded
myself that Hitler had started the war, and we too had suffered.
Our civilians in the big cities had been subjected to merciless
bombing by planes and rockets. Nazi Germany had sown the seed
and was now reaping the whirlwind: it was a country in ruins, and
one began to appreciate the enormous reconstruction and
rehabilitation task confronting the Allied occupation powers.

Back at the squadron the lads welcomed us enthusiastically,
with rumours that the next assignment for 107 Regiment was to
be in the jungles of Burma. There were whispers of pith helmets
and Burma shorts sighted in the QM stores at Brigade HQ, and
it looked as though we would soon be on our way to the Far East.
We didn't relish the thought at all: let someone else have a go,
we've done our bit, was the attitude expressed by the lads in
forthright terms to our troop officers. But inwardly we had a
feeling of resignation; realistically, now the war in Germany was
over our manpower and resources must be redeployed to end the
war with Japan.

In central Burma, Field Marshal William Slim's 14th Army had captured Mandalay and the vital communications centre of Meiktila in March, and followed up by taking Toungoo. On 3 May Rangoon was occupied unopposed, and the Burma campaign was virtually at an end. But there were considerable mopping-up operations to be carried out, and we assumed this was why our regiment was being sent out. After that, perhaps we would be included in the Allied invasion of Japan? That would be no picnic, with kamikaze pilots queuing up to achieve immortality by crashing their bomb-laden planes on to any ship afloat.

At the time it was generally recognised that Japan would eventually have to be defeated on its own soil. Japanese cities were being heavily bombed, but events had already proved that this alone does not win wars. The enemy must be defeated on the ground. Only those few privy to the secret of the terrible destruction wreaked by just one atom bomb thought otherwise.

On 25 May our CO confirmed the rumour that 107 Regiment was being sent to Burma, with the exception of men in the Age and Service Release Scheme in groups 27 and under. One could immediately deduce by their smiles those who had escaped the Burma net, and they included Tom and me in group 26, one group below the upper limit.

My diary for 28 May records: 'took tanks away to Bocholt. Last journey on the old iron horses. 64 miles. Made it in record time too!' This was a very sad day for the crews. It was like parting with old friends, and we wondered what the fate of our tanks would be in Burma. Some of the men would be reunited with them in due course, but for others it was the end of the road.

I took one last look at my beloved, battle-scarred *Buzzard* as we left her parked with hundreds of other tanks in the huge compound. The shell, bullet and shrapnel marks engraved during the battles from Normandy to Germany, clearly visible on turret and hull, brought back fleeting memories of the actions in which they were sustained. I hadn't the heart to take away the statue of the Blessed Virgin Mary I had installed in the turret by the smoke bomb ejector at Cheux, just prior to our very first battle in Normandy. It was as much a part of *Buzzard* as her guns, and I left the statue with her. It was the end. We were dehorsed!

184

In all that time, the casualty list for 34 Armoured Brigade totalled just under 1,000 of all ranks, although some recovered sufficiently to serve again. The final balance sheet for four armoured regiments in eight months of fighting was 43 officers killed and 38 seriously wounded; 199 other ranks killed and 402 seriously wounded. In the same period the regiments lost 272 Churchill tanks: 85 brewed up in action, but undoubtedly a high proportion of the other 187 were recovered later to fight again after repairs. During this time 107 Regiment was awarded one DSO (to Lieutenant Colonel Rowe, our CO); seven MCs (one awarded posthumously to Lieutenant Johnny Walker, my troop leader); one MBE; three Croix de Guerre (one for Captain Mike Hill, my troop leader); one DCM; seven MMs; 28 mentions in despatches (one awarded to my troop sergeant, A. Bradley); and 25 C-in-C certificates for gallantry or good service.

So much for the cost of our journey from the Normandy bridgehead to the east bank of the Rhine.

Chapter 19

With the British Army of Occupation in Germany

On 30 May 107 Regiment moved from Nordwalde to Munster, on wheels rather than tracks. We felt like fish out of water, but we'd have to get used to it now our life as tank crews was over. To our horror we moved into another barracks, and the lads were in a rebellious mood as they sullenly started on the old spit-and-polish routine once again. I suppose the brass knew what they were doing: perhaps, now we were the Army of Occupation, they wanted to smarten up our image as befitted the conquerors. But living in the barracks had its compensations: a bar in the canteen, a cinema hall, plenty of free time, and plenty of transport to whisk us away to other towns for dances and entertainment.

Although the non-fraternisation rule was in force in Germany, it didn't stop the black market deals and the little bits on the side. We had to keep one eye open for the authorities, of course, especially the military police. The fraus and frauleins flaunted themselves in front of us, attracted to the soldiers of the occupying army like moths to a flame. Their menfolk were either dead or in POW camps and, non-frat or not, many attempted to satisfy their sexual craving by stealth and cunning. Not that we minded! A cautious approach from a flaxen-haired beauty, with a whispered '*Guten Abend, Haben Sie Zigaretten?*', was an invitation to follow her to a secluded spot for some hanky-panky.

The lads had to watch out for the MPs whilst engaged in this nefarious activity, but the non-frat ban was self-defeating, and one wondered how long it could last. It was, as far as the troops were concerned, like putting a cream cake in front of a child and leaving the kid with a warning not to touch.

On 4 June our 'beloved' sergeant major, Donk Braybrook, was transferred to another regiment. Cheers from the lads at his departure could be heard all over Munster! Other NCOs were also moved, and by 7 June our squadron was so short that I was ordered to take the parade on the barrack square. It was my big moment, and everything went smoothly as I put the lads through the drill and left the squad standing to attention. Then, with a brisk march and an air of swank in my movements, I came to a halt in front of the CO, the crash of my boots echoing around the square. I gave the salute to Major Tapson, uttered the words, 'Parade present and correct and ready for inspection, sir,' and immediately collapsed in a heap. I was out cold!

Jock and I had gone to Enschede in Holland the previous day, and had got drunk on home-made 'hooch'. My collapse was a delayed reaction to the liquor, working on an empty stomach (I hadn't been able to face breakfast).

On 11 June Tom and I were in a detachment taking over guard duties at a Russian displaced persons camp. We had an entertaining time trying to preserve order there, but despite our efforts one Russian man was knifed in a crime of passion. They were certainly a rough mob, and had to be kept inside the compound to protect the German civilians. As it was, they had a large store of schnapps secreted away, as well as other booty gained from looting as soon as they were liberated.

In my diary I noted on 12 June, 'Got well and truly drunk on schnapps. Finished up doing Russian dances till early morning.' Just two words were noted on 13 June: 'drunk again'; on 14 June 'and again'; on 15 June, 'still on schnapps'. Nothing else was recorded in the diary until 20 June, which reads, 'Relieved by RA'. My hand was probably too shaky to write anything on the intervening days! Our high jinks occurred only when we were off duty, and we usually sobered up in time to take our turns on the duty roster. But even if there were no guards on the camp, I doubt if any of the DPs would have walked out - they were legless on schnapps most of the time we were there. Watching them perform

187

Cossack dance routines on 'rubber legs' was incredible. Their folk dancing, in which we joined, was more to our liking and less strenuous.

Apart from drinking genuine schnapps looted earlier, the Russians were distilling other alcoholic concoctions from all kinds of fermenting vegetation. We'd already received warnings about 'wood alcohol' sending some of the occupation troops blind, so we were always taking a chance when drinking the hooch. We eventually destroyed the still, as ordered by our troop officer, but with much reluctance!

On 21 June 107 Regiment completed the divide between South East Asia Command eligibles and those in the Age & Service Release Scheme, who were to remain in the Army of Occupation awaiting demobilisation. The following day official parties were laid on as a farewell celebration for the parting of the ways; one for officers, and another for the other ranks. There was another party on 23 June for all ranks of 107 Regiment RAC. These rip-roaring affairs marked the last time that whole troops, which until the end of May had lived like families, would be together before the final disbandment. Of my crew, it was sad to have to bid farewell to Joe Whelan, Owen Vaughan and Taffy Evans, who'd fought in all the battles with me in *Buzzard* since the beaches of Normandy.

There was a glimmer of hope for the SEAC eligibles when the Japanese forces in Okinawa surrendered on 22 June. The Allied navies could now cut off Japan's sea communications to the south in Burma, China and the Dutch East Indies. Wishful thinking held that Japan might surrender and 107 Regiment wouldn't have to go to the Far East.

On 25 June Tom and I were among the under 27 Age & Service contingent transferred from 107 Regiment to 147 Regiment RAC in exchange for their Far East eligibles. Another contingent was exchanged between 107 Regiment and 9th RTR in the same way. Both 147 Regiment RAC and 9th RTR thenceforth took part in the British Army of Occupation, comprising only men in the early release groups.

A shock awaited us on joining A Squadron, 147 Regiment: their new SSM was none other than Donk Braybrook, our beady-eyed sergeant-major, who had left us only three weeks ago, apparently for good. The smile on his face as he greeted us back under his wing was like that of a tiger before pouncing on its prey. Of my old troop only Bob Bolton, Kenny Rowe, Bob Garbutt and Bill Blewit were with Tom and me in A Squadron. The others in the troop, plus old friends like Tommy Reilly, Jock Gould and Bill Powland, were in different units.

The following day 147 Regiment moved to Lehre, in Brunswick, to start occupation duties on the Anglo-Russian border zone, and it became rapidly apparent that Major Lobb, the squadron CO, was no spit-and-polish martinet, much as Donk would have loved it. I made a note in my diary that it was 'pretty cushy': sufficient to be just clean and tidy, without any bull to satisfy the CO. He, like the rest of us, was simply awaiting demob, which couldn't come soon enough.

We settled in quite well with our new regiment at Lehre: there were lots of people to get to know, but the canteen was packed out on the first Friday night when Tom and I played to entertain them. Bill Powland, who managed to get a transfer to our squadron only that day, also sang some of the old favourites in his repertoire. From then until the end of the following week we had a really good time, with a party every night.

We visited a nearby Polish displaced persons camp in early July, where we found the Polish people a decent lot in comparison to the Russian DPs. They were mainly Roman Catholics, with a small minority of Jews, and were delighted when we sang our songs to them in their canteen.

On Saturday 7 July RHQ arranged a dance, to which ATS girls and Polish girls from the DP camp were invited. It was a very enjoyable evening and most of the lads were lucky with the opposite sex, including myself. A group of us escorted an equivalent number of Polish girls back to their camp, where we were given a party by the Poles in appreciation for their girls being invited to our dance. A Polish Jewess sang for us in contralto - we didn't understand a word, but the opera tunes were familiar and we joined in the choruses lustily. Bill Powland sang 'O Sole

Mio' in a duet with her, and they harmonised beautifully, albeit in different tongues.

On 8 July our squadron moved from Lehre to mount guard duties on the Anglo-Russian frontier zone at Radenbeck, near Brome. We were under strict orders not to stray across the boundary, marked by white tape, which stretched for miles. The penalty for disobeying this order was probably court martial, but we were never tempted: we didn't fancy getting shot up by the Russkies, and only ventured up to the border to take our turns as frontier guards. We viewed the Russian guards with reciprocated suspicion. They looked like Mongolians, and compared with our smart dress, enhanced by blanco webbings and polished brass, they were a scruffy lot.

If the penalty for our troops caught in the Russian zone was severe, it was nothing compared to that exacted by the Russians on their troops caught in our zone, if appearances were anything to go by. Two Russian soldiers in a drunken stupor were picked up by our lads well our side of the border, and guarded at squadron HQ while negotiations took place with the Russian authorities. A Russian escort arrived to take them back, and I was in the office when the officer in charge arrived. He could speak English, and when our officer enquired what punishment the men might receive, the Russian tapped his revolver and put his hand to his head, his right index finger on his temple and thumb outstretched. There was no doubt at all that they would be shot. Our grumbles about conditions and a little bit of bull suddenly seemed rather insignificant.

With the non-fraternisation ban in force, we were finding things very difficult indeed. Our squadron had taken over Radenbeck completely, including some empty houses, so we managed to make ourselves comfortable despite having to sleep on the floor. But we were living among the German people for the first time, and although they didn't exactly kow-tow to us, they tried to ingratiate themselves all the time. We were allowed to speak to or play around only with the children; but when we did it was hard to refrain from talking to their mothers as well. For their part, they wouldn't have minded us playing around with them too! It was a relief when Monty eased the non-fraternisation restriction on 14 July.

With the lifting of the ban it was quite in order to talk to the local townsfolk, using sign language and a mixture of English and German. They were really grateful to be allowed to converse with us, and showed their appreciation in many ways. In the cafe we went to that night, we were made to feel like their saviours in keeping the Russians at a safe distance: they were absolutely terrified after hearing reports of Red Army rape and pillage. They were saddened, too, at what might happen to their relatives in the Russian zone.

The German civilians also took great delight in debunking Hitler. Freedom of speech had been restored, and they were making the most of it. A poster of the Führer, with the message, 'Ein Reich, Ein Volk, Ein Führer', hung on the wall of the café, scribbled all over with rude German graffiti and spat upon by the locals. We were almost convinced that the Germans were sincere in their rejection of Hitler and the whole Nazi ideology. Germany was a ruined country, and they seemed genuine in their desire to atone for Nazi sins and co-operate with the western powers in bringing democracy to the zones under their control. But, heeding Monty's warning in his original non-fraternisation regulations, we had reservations about the sincerity of their protestations against Hitler and the Nazis. Time alone would tell, but in the meanwhile we gave them the benefit of the doubt.

With the fraternisation ban ended there was no further need for clandestine meetings with German fraus and frauleins, and when the café closed at night there was no lack of escorts to walk home with the women. I accompanied a girl called Maria, and it was nice to be able to consort with a girl without having to look over your shoulder or feel guilty about contravening regulations.

The following night it was my good fortune to meet a very attractive girl named Betty. She was about my own age, we took a liking to each other right away, and she became my regular girlfriend for the rest of the two months we stayed at Radenbeck. She had fled her home in the Russian zone and now occupied a ground floor room in a communal house. Her husband had fought

191

and died on the eastern front and her relatives were in the Russian zone, so she was all alone. After walking her home for a few nights, she allowed me into her room. It was a cloak and dagger affair, as it was dangerous for both of us to be caught. In my case, I would be put on a charge for contravening regulations banning us from entering German houses; in Betty's, she would be turned out by the owner, who lived on the premises.

I gained a quick entry into her room at night without going through the front door by climbing through the window. Betty, inside, would quietly lift up the sash, and I would remove my boots and pass them up to her before heaving myself in over the head-high window ledge. When I left I went through the same procedure in reverse, putting my boots back on again when I reached the pavement beneath the window. I could tiptoe about the room in my socks, avoiding the sounds made by army boots on a hard floor - something of a give-away in the still of the night!

Back on guard duty on the Anglo-Russian border, the Russian guards had the more difficult job, in that they had to apprehend anyone endeavouring to flee to the British zone. It was one-way traffic, since no one wanted to go in the opposite direction!

It was the beginning of what Churchill designated the Iron Curtain, and we turned a blind eye to anyone who succeeded in evading the Russian patrols and entering our zone. Only a few managed to trickle through, and those who did were obviously desperate enough to chance being shot by the Russian guards. We could hear shots now and again over the border, proving that the Russians were trigger-happy and wouldn't hesitate to shoot anyone caught trying to cross the frontier and escape to the west. At all times we kept a distance between us and the Russian guards. The distrust was mutual.

Back with the regiment, Tom and I both got into a scrape: he punched a sergeant in a fracas, and got arrested; I was awoken from a drunken sleep at Betty's to be taken to squadron HQ after the incident and, confusedly thinking I would be wrongly implicated in the affair, abused Donk roundly and got arrested too. Tom was remanded in custody for a Field General Court Martial, and I was busted to the ranks and ordered to serve 14 days in detention.

I believe our harsh punishment was due to a general crack-down by the army top brass, given the lack of discipline among the troops now the war was at an end in Germany. Most of the lads were drinking heavily to alleviate the boredom of occupation duties, which led, inevitably, to fighting among themselves. We were fed up: we'd finished the job for which we had been conscripted, and now we just wanted to go home.

Tom and I were taken to RHQ at the Lehre barracks, and put behind bars in a dark, damp, underground cell, with just a little daylight coming through the top part of a barred window protruding above the outside pavement level. My eyes became accustomed to the dimness of the cell, and I saw it contained just three palliasses on wooden platforms, with a couple of folded blankets on each. Nothing else. I had only 14 days to tolerate, but Tom could be facing a much longer sentence in this dingy hole. He circumvented some of his punishment by reporting sick the next morning: he must have put on a good act, because the MO ordered him to be sent to hospital for tests and observation. He came back five days later, gleefully boasting of comfortable beds, pretty nurses and good food.

In his absence, I was put on cookhouse fatigues for the first two days, and made to work hard for the next three cleaning up the concert hall. The worst part was the solitary confinement at night, with the exception of one night when I had a companion. My cell-mate was charged with being AWOL for six weeks, shacking up with a woman in Munster, and was discharged from the army with ignominy the following morning. When he collected his kit from our cell after the verdict he seemed quite happy at the outcome, treating it as a reward rather than a punishment.

On 6 August Tom was charged with the assault on the NCO, and sentenced to 21 days field punishment. In the event he reported sick again the next morning, and this time he wasn't malingering. He had severe gastroenteritis, and was sent to hospital to see out the 21 days. At the finish he rejoined our squadron instead of going back into detention – lucky old Tom! In contrast, on the morning of Tom's trial I reported sick with a rash on my body, but was only ordered to see the medics at the barracks for daily treatment. It was back to solitary confinement in the cell at nights, until my release on 10 August.

Chapter 20

A Christmas to Remember

The first atom bomb was dropped on Hiroshima on 6 August 1945, an event which overshadowed everything else worldwide. While we were still assimilating details of the awesome destructive powers of one single bomb, the Americans dropped the second atom bomb on the port city of Nagasaki on 9 August. The massive, almost total, devastation of both cities with countless casualties was difficult to comprehend at the time. But everybody was agreed that Japan must now surrender to prevent further bombing; and, sure enough, on 14 August Emperor Hirohito agreed to accept unconditional surrender terms dictated by the Allies.

The day after I returned to my squadron, Donk lost no time in putting me back on frontier guard for a 48-hour tour of duty. But my body rash, which I thought was perhaps the result of an ill-advised amorous conquest, became worse, and I eventually had to be admitted for dermatological treatment at Brunswick hospital. I was in for a surprise when I reached the hospital, as who did I spy in a ward there but brother Tom, looking fit and well, and very surprised but happy to see me.

Later that day, after bidding goodbye to Tom, I was sent to 121 British General Hospital in Brunswick. In the next bed was a fellow Londoner, Bill Ellis, from West Ham; having a lot in common, we got on very well. This was the first time I'd been in hospital, and it was paradise compared to the conditions I'd recently experienced in detention. It was sheer luxury to lie in bed with the headphones on, listening to Glenn Miller on the radio.

195

The famous USAAF band leader had disappeared on a flight to Paris in December 1944, and no trace of the plane or its occupants was ever found. Since then, the airwaves were full of Glenn Miller records in tribute to the great musician and the unique sound of his band.

The dermatology specialist examined my body rash, which was by then fairly extensive and unpleasant: my whole torso was completely covered in scaly sores. He reassured me that it would clear up after a week or ten days of treatment, and informed me that I was suffering from psoriasis caused by sulphur poisoning, rather than any more unspeakable disease.

The news everybody was waiting for arrived at the hospital on 24 August: demob was at hand, but only 23 Age and Service Group were to be released by the end of the year. It came as a terrible shock: hardly anybody in the hospital was in the 23 Group and under. It was enough to give us all a relapse. Harsh words were directed towards the Labour Party and Attlee, the new Prime Minister , in particular. A lot of the forces had voted Labour solely as a result of reports that demobilisation would be quicker under them than the Tories.

Demobilisation was the one topic, above anything else, guaranteed to raise the blood pressure: everybody wanted out, and the sooner the better. The Second World War was over, we'd all done our bit, and just wanted to get back home into civvy life again. Yet here we were, carrying out boring Army of Occupation duties, and being treated as if we were part of the regular army. But with so many writing home complaining about the spit-and-polish, it wasn't long before the newspapers directed their venom at the brass hats responsible for the harsh discipline imposed upon the men.

I was discharged from hospital on 29 August and returned to my unit at Radenbeck - it was great to be back at last with Tom and all the other lads. We missed the lovely singing of Bill Powland, who was taken ill while on compassionate leave to see his sick father and never returned from England (he was eventually demobbed back at home), but otherwise it was just like old times again. Things weren't too bad under Sergeant Harris, the acting

SSM who took over when Donk was transferred to RHQ, and who had no further ambition than to get out as soon as possible, like the rest of us.

On 2 September Tom and I were included in a detachment to take over guard duties at a military hospital at Gifhorn. The patients and staff were German, and an army guard would not normally be necessary, but we found to our disgust that some wards housed injured jailers from the notorious Belsen concentration camp. They bore the scars of retribution inflicted by their former victims after liberation by the British. One might feel sympathy for the German soldier wounded in action, but we had only utter contempt for Josef Kramer's thugs, who took part in the torture and killing of many thousands of prisoners.

By the looks of it, the former prisoners had wreaked a terrible vengeance; but one man was virtually unscathed, although he deserved more punishment than most. Doctor Klein was kept in a room separate from the others, and was one of the original doctors at the gruesome Auschwitz extermination camp, where he participated in Mengele's inhuman medical experiments. I saw Klein many times whilst on guard outside his room, when he was taken under armed escort to be interrogated. He was a big man, but deceptively mild-looking, and it seemed inconceivable that he had carried out diabolical experiments on human beings. We were told by an intelligence sergeant that Klein had even made lamp-shades from human skin.

After returning from Gifhorn I was ordered to report to the squadron CO, Major Lobb, on Sunday 9 September. I had no idea what it could be about, and felt rather apprehensive, as the last time I saw him the Major had sentenced me to 14 days' detention. Now, it seemed, he wanted my co-operation. 'Corporal Powland won't be returning from the UK, and I need a replacement squadron clerk. Would you be agreeable to doing the job for me? I see by your records that you were a purchasing clerk in civilian life, and I'm sure you could manage it.' I felt like telling him to stuff the job, but then reflected on the great advantages of the position and accepted the post of A Squadron clerk. It was cushy street for me thenceforth, although I don't think I would have accepted if SSM Donk Braybrook hadn't been transferred to RHQ. I got on very well, though, with Sergeant Harris, the acting SSM.

I got stuck into the clerical work, with a little guidance and tuition from the duty officer. There was a lot of catching up to do and I was kept quite busy, but my one-finger typing stood me in good stead. I managed to type squadron orders that day, and saw Tom was included in the next 48-hour frontier guard for the following morning. There, but for my new office job, I would have gone too. I was, as Tom said, a 'jammy sod': I now had every evening free, and finished up with Betty each night after drinks at a café or beer house.

On 19 September the squadron moved to Meinersen: Betty was in tears as she waved goodbye, as were a lot of the other fraus and frauleins. We'd been stationed at Radenbeck for nearly three months, and close attachments had developed between the lads and the women, so it was a sad farewell as the convoy of trucks drove away.

For Tom and me it was hardly worth unpacking, as we were due to go on UK leave the following day, and only had time for a quick look round before turning in ready for an early start next morning. We left Meinersen on Thursday 20 September and travelled to a transit camp at Hanover, where we met some lads en route to the Harz Mountain, a holiday centre run by the British army for the troops. By all accounts it was a sort of paradise, and some troops preferred to spend their leave there rather than go back to the UK, but no inducement would entice Tom and me to give up our nine days' leave in Bethnal Green - our Shangri La in the East End of London.

The whole family was at home to greet us, and the excitement was heightened by Mum waving a telegram as we walked in. Bob, our elder brother, had been with the forces in Hong Kong when it was captured by the Japanese, and we hadn't heard a word since - not even if he was dead or alive. The telegram which ended years of worry by giving us the news that he was safe had arrived just one hour before. What a marvellous start to our leave!

We went back to Germany on 4 October, docking at the Hook

of Holland before boarding a troop train to Hanover. During the long journey the train came to a halt on a bridge above a road in Rotterdam. As we looked out we could see some children waving to us, so Tom pulled the window down and threw a few sweets to them. Other lads joined in, and within minutes there were hundreds of kids scrabbling about, picking up our parcels of sandwiches, sweets and chocolate. The Pied Piper of Hamelin himself couldn't have brought the kids out so quickly: they'd undoubtedly gone short under the German occupation, and it gave us great pleasure to distribute the goodies.

Later on, at a stop at a German station, Tom pulled a fast one on a German black marketeer. He was among many on the platform bartering with the troops, and offered us a camera, but no one had sufficient currency, cigarettes, coffee and suchlike to meet his demands. Then, just as the train started to move off, Tom snatched the camera and closed the window, leaving the startled man to run alongside the train gesticulating and shouting until he had to stop at the end of the platform. The cheeky, thieving Tom then pulled down the window, popped his head out, and held up the camera to pretend he was taking a snapshot of the man left stranded on the station. I heard the shutter click, but unfortunately there was no film in it - what a souvenir that picture would have been! Tom's booty was an Agfa 120 folding camera.

We rejoined our unit on Saturday 6 October, and found things had been happening in Meinersen: 147 Regiment was being disbanded, with its demise programmed to be completed by the end of October. On 10 October our A Squadron CO, Major Lobb, gave a dinner and party for all ranks to celebrate his demobilisation the following day. Everybody had a great time and the booze flowed freely.

On 19 October Tom and I and a couple of other lads were invited to a German wedding party in Meinersen. The wedding reception was a lavish affair, with a sumptuous meal and an amazing selection of cakes and pastries. Tom and I played the music as wine flowed and beer and schnapps was poured liberally by our German hosts. We had a really smashing time, and the bride and groom thanked us for helping the party to go with a swing. The groom, a young German soldier, was a nice lad, and it was hard to imagine that only a few months ago we would have been filled with hatred for each other as we fought on opposing sides. The couple had a living good luck symbol at their wedding, in the shape of the local chimney sweep in his working clothes, complete with top hat.

Non-fraternisation was gradually becoming a thing of the past: British troops were mixing freely with the German people and discovering that, basically, they were similar in most respects to our own people. My girlfriend at the time, Emily, was Aryan in type and had all the attributes any man could desire!

On Sunday 21 October Tom and I went to another wedding: one of the lads in our squadron, Joe Sampson, was getting married. He was a Jew and had chosen for his bride the Polish Jewess who entertained us with her wonderful singing at the DP camp at Lehre. The wedding ceremony, which was conducted by a rabbi in Brunswick, was a rather spectacular affair: the bride and groom stood together under a four-sided draped canopy, with a man at each corner holding a pole to support it. At the culmination of the service toasts were drunk to Joe and his wife. The couple responded by drinking the wine and then throwing their glasses to smash with a tinkle in the fireplace. I could barely refrain from laughing as Tom whispered into my ear, 'You can't blame 'em, the wine tasted like vinegar anyway!'

A week later I had the most wonderful surprise when I received a letter postmarked from Bethnal Green and addressed in my brother Bob's handwriting. Imagine my excitement as I quickly tore open the envelope and started to read its contents, with Tom standing by waiting for me to pass the pages on after I'd finished. Bob had arrived back in England on 18 October, and said nothing of the terrible ordeals he had suffered during his imprisonment, but was full of praise for the wonderful treatment he'd received from the Americans whilst en route from his prison camp in Osaka. He told us he was now fit and well and back to normal weight. This marvellous news from Bob was an extra cause to celebrate in the café that night.

Drafts were leaving for demob at regular intervals, and by 6

November 147 Regiment was reduced to a skeleton. Acting RSM Donk Braybrook was on the draft which left that day: he really wasn't such a bad guy, and after a good old booze-up he was a bit emotional when he bade goodbye personally to us few left from 107 Regiment. Tom and I had served under him in B Squadron since the early days back in Kent in 1943.

On 12 November the depleted 147 Regiment RAC was concentrated at Fallersleben. We'd been at Meinersen for two months: the people had been good to us during our stay there, and as our convoy moved off they came out on the streets and waved us goodbye. Who would have thought that our erstwhile enemy would be sorry to see us depart from their midst!

By the following day 147 Regiment had been completely disbanded and all personnel posted to various other units. During the two days at Fallersleben some of us took the opportunity of visiting the giant Volkswagen motors plant, only about four miles away at Wolfsburg. It was a huge place and well worth seeing - our official guided tour of the complex included tea and cakes. Next day Tom and I and a few others were despatched to Hanover and posted to the 5th Reconnaissance Regiment RAC, stationed in the Hanoverian suburb of Herrenhausen. We were billeted in an apartment block a couple of miles from the centre of Hanover, and settled in quite comfortably.

Apart from odd guard duties, things were very easy here. The unit had completely taken over a local beer house for use as a canteen, where Tom and I performed on the piano for the lads and became popular immediately. There was also a dance hall nearby, with a good band of German civilian instrumentalists. The hall was large, the floor good to dance on, the frauleins pretty and, apart from the language barrier, it was like twirling girls around at the Hammersmith Palais.

The unit did everything to make the last months of our army service as pleasant as possible, and I was given a job in the squadron office to replace a clerk leaving for demob. Prior to that I had done only two guard duties at the main railway station in Hanover, the Haupt-Bahnhof, where our job was to patrol the underground bunkers and keep order amongst the masses of people made homeless by Allied bombing raids. Like most big German cities, Hanover had suffered heavily from wartime raids, but the Germans were already working like beavers on the task of reconstruction.

It's remarkable how breweries, like churches, often survived the bombing raids; I noticed this in both Germany and the East End of London. On Herrenhausen Straat a brewery had escaped damage in the bombing, and it was inevitable that with our experience of gaining entry into Mann Crossmans brewery at Whitechapel we would try it on here. Successfully, as it turned out: Tom and I with a couple of others knocked beer back until the early hours on two December nights in the Herrenhausen Straat brewery.

We had more good news from home: Mum wrote to tell us that the BBC planned to broadcast a family reunion party at the first post-war Christmas, to be included in a round-the-world programme on Christmas Day culminating in the speech by His Majesty King George VI. With Bob recently returned from internment in a Japanese POW camp, the Dysons would be the ideal family to take part in the programme if the twins could get leave from Germany. Mum accepted the proposition, after Bob assured her that the War Office would grant special leave for Tom and me, and Bob himself wrote to ask for this. We were cock-a-hoop to think we'd been chosen to represent a typical British family reunion, and that it would be broadcast worldwide.

I was doing some paperwork in the squadron office on 12 December when the CO called me into his room and showed me a directive from the War Office. Troopers S. Dyson and T. Dyson were to proceed on leave, to arrive in the UK on 16 December and depart back for Germany on 30 December, in order to take part in a BBC programme to be broadcast on Christmas Day. The CO was most impressed when I explained the story to him, and promised to publicise our broadcast so the whole squadron could listen in. Two days later Tom and I left Hanover.

On 16 December all the Dyson family were together for the first time since 1936, and celebrated the occasion accordingly. Looking at Bob, I could hardly believe it was nine years since I'd last seen him. He seemed to be quite fit, and had hardly changed in appearance – it was incredible that he'd recovered so well from the inhuman treatment he suffered for so long in the Jap POW camps. Bob told us more of his ordeals that night than he ever did afterwards. It was all so fresh in his mind, but he had survived the starvation, sickness, beatings and utter degradation heaped upon him during nearly four years in captivity.

The next day we three brothers sallied forth to the West End and painted the town red. Bob was then 37, seven years older than us twins, and determined to make up for the lost years of his life. Pockets bulging with money, we went on a glorious binge to celebrate Bob's safe return. It was a wonderful day.

On 18 December the BBC engineers arrived at our home to install the equipment for the Christmas broadcast. Each member of the family was given a script, and we went through rehearsals. Not surprisingly life was chaotic: what with the BBC people around and a family to cook for, it was very hard on Mum, although she seemed to thrive on it. One item off the menu was rice pudding, though; I don't suppose Bob has eaten a grain of his staple diet as a POW since being liberated.

With all the outside broadcasting equipment already installed at our house, the BBC took the opportunity to include an item on the East End's reaction to the first peacetime Christmas in the 'In Town Tonight' programme, talking to people in the street market outside our home. The presenter was Wynford Vaughan-Thomas, the war correspondent. Having covered battles in Europe for the BBC, he was very interested to hear about the actions Tom and I took part in with 107 Regiment, and the best place to talk over things was in the White Hart, just across the road from where he was to conduct the broadcast. Wynford was a jovial and interesting character, and we soon discovered he was also generous. He insisted on paying for a crate of pale ale to take back with us after closing time, and paid for a round of drinks in the pub. Sixteen cherry brandies!

Every night was party night that week, and it all proved too much for Mum: on Saturday 22 December she was rushed into Bethnal Green Hospital to be treated for an internal haemorrhage after collapsing at home. Poor old Dad was devastated, but cheered up when he was told that Mum's condition was not too serious. She needed a complete rest, and was detained in hospital under observation.

Mum's illness certainly put a damper on things, and the party intended for that night was abandoned. We didn't feel like dancing in the streets and just settled for a quiet drink at home with our family and friends. We thought it would probably put paid to our Christmas broadcast, though that was unimportant compared to Mum's health. But the next day, when Bob telephoned the BBC to tell them what had happened, they decided the Dyson family broadcast would still go on the air, but with Eileen starting the broadcast instead of Mum. Revised scripts would be prepared, and a rehearsal would take place the following day, Christmas Eve. The best news of all was that Mum would finish off the broadcast, speaking from her hospital bed.

On Christmas morning we were all up bright and early. Bob organised things almost on military lines, from the preparation of breakfast to the tidying up afterwards, to ensure everything was spick and span before the BBC crew arrived. The broadcast began with the chimes of Big Ben striking the hour at 2.00pm, followed by an introduction from the London studio and contributions from civilians and servicemen all around England and across the world. The penultimate item, prior to the King's Christmas message, was the Dyson family reunion Christmas party.

Howard Marshall, the presenter, introduced us: 'From France back to Britain. From the ruins of Caen and the white crosses of Bayeux we move again to London. To London's East End, still bearing in its little streets the mark of its long ordeal by fire and bomb and rocket. We're calling on a house in Bethnal Green, 376 Bethnal Green Road, the home of the Dyson family, to speak for all the thousands of families in Britain today who are spending a Christmas of peace together for the first time since war began.'

Eileen introduced our family, and we each said a few words about how much the Christmas party meant to us. Then we heard Mum's voice, coming over loud and clear through the BBC radio monitor in our lounge, telling us she was feeling fine, and that we were to carry on with the party and enjoy ourselves. She thanked the doctors and nursing staff at the hospital for the way she was being treated, and wished all the families in the country being reunited after the war a Merry Christmas.

We listened to the Christmas message to the nation given by His Majesty King George VI, and you could have heard a pin drop at the end of the speech before the radio monitor was switched off. Then there was uproar in our lounge! The BBC crew congratulated us on an 'super broadcast' and had a few farewell drinks before dismantling their equipment and departing; while the Dyson family party started right there and then.

Following our broadcast and the publicity given to it in the national press, we received shoals of letters from people in England and overseas. The impact on listeners was heightened by the fact that Mum was rushed into hospital just a couple of days before Christmas, and hearing Mum speaking from the hospital tugged at their heartstrings. Bob's story also aroused the emotions. Hardly had we got over our hangovers on Boxing Day than journalists from the national press descended upon us. We featured in a major story in the *Daily Herald* the next day, complete with a picture of Mum in her hospital bed, and another of us gathered round the piano at home. There was also a cartoon by Gilbert Wilkinson, depicting our lounge after the party with Mum cleaning up the mess.

All in all it was a family reunion to remember.

Epilogue

Tom and I were due to return to Hanover on 30 December, but applied to the RTO as usual for an extension of leave. This time we were able to put a copy of the *Daily Herald* in front of him as incontrovertible proof that our mother was ill! Mum was finally discharged from hospital, fit and well again, on 13 January, and Tom and I went back to Hanover on 15 January, knowing it would only be a matter of a few weeks before our demob. We were treated as celebrities by our unit, as most of them had heard the Dyson family reunion party broadcast on Christmas Day.

We made the most of the remaining weeks at Hanover, with plenty of night-life, dances, parties, booze and birds, so it all passed quickly. On Saturday 23 February a farewell party was held for the 26 A & S group; then, on the Monday, we were transferred to 33 RFT holding unit at a barracks to wait our turn to be transported back to the UK.

At last, on 4 March, we started on our journey back into civilian life. We landed at Harwich on the morning of 5 March 1946, and on arrival in London were given the choice of keeping our army uniform or handing it back in exchange for civilian clothes. Somebody had a sense of humour!

Our draft, only too anxious to swap their khaki for a blue pin-stripe suit, was taken to a military dispersal unit in Olympia to effect the transformation from squaddie to civvy on the conveyor-belt principle. Tailors' dummies were displayed in a large hall, dressed in various styles of civvy suits, overcoats and hats. We were invited to inspect the clothing, rather like going into a department store, and each individual was measured and given his chosen outfit. I picked a double-breasted blue suit and grey trilby hat; Tom opted for a single-breasted grey suit and a dark blue trilby. We looked even less like twins than when we were in uniform.

We were each given our Soldiers Release Book, which contains a 'testimonial to the soldier' on the back page. Mine read: 'Military Conduct: Exemplary. Testimonial: Trooper S. Dyson has done nearly six years service, during which time he has proved himself competent and hardworking. During the battle he was an operator in a tank. Lately he has been clerking and this job he has performed absolutely satisfactorily. He can be entrusted with confidential matters, as he is discreet and trustworthy. He is cheerful and easy to work with. He is sober and of excellent character.'

That's what you get for six years in the army!